IRAN AND ITS PLACE AMONG NATIONS

IRAN AND ITS PLACE AMONG NATIONS

Alidad Mafinezam and
Aria Mehrabi

Westport, Connecticut
London

Library of Congress Cataloging-in-Publication Data

Mafinezam, Alidad.
　Iran and its place among nations / Alidad Mafinezam and Aria Mehrabi.
　　p. cm.
　Includes bibliographical references and index.
　ISBN 978–0–275–99926–1 (alk. paper)
　1. Iran—Politics and government—20th century.　2. Iran—Foreign relations.
3. Geopolitics—Iran.　4. Iran—Economic policy.　5. East and West.　I. Mehrabi, Aria.　II. Title.
　DS318.M315　2008
　327.55–dc22　　　2007029919

British Library Cataloguing in Publication Data is available.

Library of Congress Catalog Card Number: 2007029919
ISBN-13: 978–0–275–99926–1

First published in 2008

Praeger Publishers, 88 Post Road West, Westport, CT 06881
An imprint of Greenwood Publishing Group, Inc.
www.praeger.com

Printed in the United States of America

The paper used in this book complies with the
Permanent Paper Standard issued by the National
Information Standards Organization (Z39.48–1984).

10 9 8 7 6 5 4 3 2 1

Contents

Acknowledgments

The authors would like to thank the following individuals for their ideas and support in the writing of this book. In Toronto, Mr. Vahan Kololian, Professor Reza Baraheni, Ms. Leili Pourzand, Dr. Mehrdad Hariri, and Mr. Ali Ehsassi deserve special mention. In New York, Professor Richard Bulliet and Dr. Hossein Kamaly gave generously of their time. In Maryland, Mr. Ardeshir Lotfalian's advice was highly valuable. The impetus for writing this book came from a conversation with Mr. Afshin Molavi, which took place in the spring of 2005 at Kramer Books and Afterwords Café in the Dupont Circle area of Washington, DC. The wise counsel of Ms. Hilary Claggett, senior editor at Praeger Publishers, has been indispensable. We are thankful to them all.

Introduction

Few countries in the world are as newsworthy as the Islamic Republic of Iran. In the past two years, especially, from the summer of 2005 onward, Iran has been in the international headlines on an almost daily basis, giving the impression that it is one of the most important countries in the world. To be sure, almost all of the news about Iran has been negative, as major powers, led by the United States, have continually expressed alarm over Iran's nuclear program, its growing influence in neighboring Iraq, and its moral and material support for anti-Israel, Islamist groups in the Palestinian territories and Lebanon. The war of words shows no signs of abating, as Iran's populist president, Mahmoud Ahmadinejad, with the nod of the country's supreme leader, Seyed Ali Khamenei, rails against what he sees as the injustices of the current international order, and takes his harsh rhetoric and his message of defiance to the far-flung corners of Iran and to every country he visits in the developing world, as well as the floor of the United Nations in New York. All of the world's main industrialized countries, loathe to host the Iranian president in their capitals, look on in shock and dismay, wondering how the Iranian government hopes to improve the lot of its people when it rejects the foundations of the current international order, from which it wishes to draw sustenance and know-how. How can Iran develop, many wonder, when its leaders' favorite pastime is lashing out at the most powerful and advanced countries in the world?

In the eyes of the United States and numerous leading European countries, Iran is indeed the black sheep of the international community. Apart from a brief visit by then Italian prime minister Romano Prodi in the summer of 1997, in the final months of his tenure, no head of state from the elite G8 has visited postrevolutionary Iran. In the North American and European press, Iran continues to be portrayed as a source of instability and radicalism in a vitally important part of the world. The acute sense of worry about Iran's intentions has culminated in successive United Nations Security Council sanctions resolutions against Iran, aimed at imposing stiff restrictions on all entities and individuals who cooperate with the country's nuclear program. The latest of these has been the UNSC resolution 1737, which was unanimously passed on March 25, 2007. To observers of international affairs, the question remains: is Iran destined to remain as a real or perceived source of regional and international problems, or can a way be found to productively integrate it into the international system? Are Iran and the United States destined to remain as adversaries, or is it possible for them to chart a more cooperative course for their own and the international community's benefit?

This book is written in response to these questions in an attempt to bring the much-needed perspective to the debate surrounding Iran and its rightful place among the community of nations. It is written in a particularly tense period in Iran's international relations, when the danger of military conflict and the specter of even greater conflagration in the Middle East remain haunting. Looking beyond and beneath today's headlines, this book attempts to address the broad question of why Iran is important to the international community, and why the success or failure of its integration into regional and international arrangements will have consequences that far transcend the country itself. This book attempts to place Iran's current predicament in context by examining where the country has been, where it is today, and where it may ideally end up in the future. Is Iran destined to remain a source of rebellion and rejection of the international order, or can it in fact become an anchor of stability in the region that surrounds it, in the Muslim world, and beyond?

More than an academic exercise, this book is written with a pragmatic intent to see how ways can be found out of the current deadlock, in hopes that a peaceful resolution of Iran's disputes with the major international players can benefit the Iranian people and others. It is the key assumption of this book that deep understanding and knowledge are the mainstays of the search for solutions. To see how the current difficulties can be overcome, we feel it is necessary to break out of the chain of name-calling and reactionary politics that have characterized much of Iran's and its adversaries' mind-sets, especially in their bilateral encounters. This is especially true of Iran's relationship with the United States.

It is indeed becoming increasingly untenable for Iranian leaders to blame their problems on foreign plots and Western conspiracies. From the other end of the spectrum, Iran's adversaries—the United States and Israel chief among them—must make a genuine effort to understand where Iran is coming from, and where the sources of its grievances lie; it will no longer suffice to blame Iran's actions merely on the fanatical and antidemocratic leanings of its leaders. Thus far, the chain of reaction has precluded constructive action regarding Iran. Name-calling and catch-all phrases—such as "terrorist," "rogue," "evil," and "fundamentalist" from one direction, and "imperialist," "usurper," "world arrogance," and "bully" from the other—have overshadowed genuine quests for reconciliation. Knowledge and understanding about Iran by the world, and about the world by Iran, are indispensable remedies to the current predicament. This book hopes to provide a basic, albeit much-needed step in that direction.

From a humanitarian standpoint, the importance of Iran has to do with the current condition, and the hopes and aspirations of the 70 million people who live there. Ever since the revolution of 1979, which overturned the millennial tradition of monarchy, the collective will of Iranians to build better lives for themselves and their children has encountered major obstacles. The eight-year Iran–Iraq war of the 1980s, which was started by Saddam Hussein, was devastating to the country as it cost Iran hundreds of thousands of lives and hundreds of billions of dollars in economic damage. Close to two decades after the end of what Iranian officials call the "imposed war," the process of building Iran continues in fits and starts. The U.S. policy of containing and weakening Iran has indisputably exacerbated the economic condition of the Iranian people.

This state of affairs has instilled among Iranians a broad sense of disgruntlement and feelings of dejection, which have been directed partially at their own government, and partially at foreign countries. Economic growth in postrevolutionary Iran has indeed been sporadic at best. Joblessness, inflation, drug abuse, extreme urban air pollution, and a general sense among the country's burgeoning youth and the middle class that they lack prospects for progress, have further fuelled this broad-based sense of discontent. In the postrevolutionary period millions of educated Iranians have left Iran for industrialized countries where their hopes and talents can be put to use. To make matters worse, since the mid-1990s Iran has been subject to comprehensive U.S. sanctions that have worked to devalue Iran's currency, and have deterred large-scale investment in Iran by the main sources of international capital. Mere sustenance has become a daily struggle for the average Iranian, as stagnant wages have forced many to work double or triple shifts to make ends meet. This state of affairs is unsustainable because the general feelings of discontent feed the power of reactionary politicians who blame all of Iran's problems on the country's "enemies."

The feelings of discontent among the country's youth—close to 45 million Iranians, of a population of 70 million, are below the age of 30—are indirectly channeled beyond Iran's borders, as they provide fodder for adventurous Iranian policies in Iraq, the greater Middle East, and beyond. In this sense, Iran matters not only for the people who live there, but for other countries that are influenced by its actions. It is thus impossible to discuss Iran's place in the world without at the same time discussing its domestic condition in its economic, cultural, political, and geostrategic dimensions.

From a strategic and geopolitical standpoint, Iran's importance is easy to grasp. Even a cursory glance at the world's map shows that Iran is located at the very centre of Central Eurasia, an area in which all the world's major power blocks—America, Europe, and Asia—have vital interests, and the only part of the world over which the major power blocks often compete, especially since it contains a major portion of the world's oil and gas reserves. Connecting the Persian Gulf to the Caspian Sea, Iran is the geopolitical and cultural nerve center of a region of vital importance to the international community. Its stability will harmonize the region that surrounds it; its instability will export disorder and chaos.

To elucidate this point, we refer to the work of Zbigniew Brzezinski, one of the most astute American strategic thinkers of the past generation, whose grasp of practical policymaking is matched by his academic understanding of international relations. Having served as National Security Advisor to President Jimmy Carter, and having authored numerous groundbreaking works on the global balance of power, he has discussed Iran's strategic importance in detail in two of his books, *The Grand Chessboard: American Primacy and Its Geo-strategic Imperatives*, which came out in 1997; and *The Choice: Global Domination or Global Leadership*, which appeared in 2004.[1] At the very beginning of the *Grand Chessboard*, Brzezinski writes: "Ever since the continents started interacting politically, some five hundred years ago, Eurasia has been at the center of world power . . . Not only is its [Eurasia's] western periphery—Europe—still the location of much of the world's political and economic power, but its eastern region—Asia—has lately become a vital center of economic growth and rising political influence."[2]

In discussing "geopolitical pivots," *The Grand Chessboard* features a map of "The Global Zone of Percolating Violence." This map, which, in Brzezinski's thinking, constitutes the most strategically significant part of the world, includes the Middle East, the Caucasus, and Central Asia. Iran, in Brzezinski's formulation, falls at the very center of this vitally important area, and connects these three regions. It has the potential, as the most populous and historically entrenched country in the region, to serve as a potent anchor of stability.[3] Similarly, in his subsequent book, *The Choice*, Brzezinski discusses the benefits of Iran's "global integration," with a focus on economic development and stability in Iran and the region that surrounds it. In this book he discusses the fact that Iran—if it can transcend its lingering reactionary revolutionary ideology—has all the national attributes to make it a positive influence in an unstable and potentially explosive region.[4]

Discussing Iran's strategic significance is especially relevant now, in the year 2007, as American and allied military forces are stationed in significant numbers in Iraq and in Afghanistan, both of which share long borders with Iran. In this sense, especially, Iran and America are "neighbors" who can no longer safely ignore one another. Here are some of the most important reasons for Iran's heightened strategic importance to the United States and other major powers.

Iraq. With 150,000 American forces bogged down in a country wracked by ethnic and religious divisions, Iran has the potential to make positive contributions to Iraq's stability, economic development, and its territorial integrity, in hopes that the tragic, war-induced violence that has claimed hundreds of thousands of Iraqi lives since the American-led invasion in 2003 can be brought under control. In this area, in particular, Iran's ability dwarfs that of any other regional power. Since the two-term presidency of George W. Bush will largely be judged by the extent of its success in stabilizing Iraq, it is safe to assume that Iran's strategic significance for the United States is greater than it has ever been. Another key issue in Iraq is the fate of the Kurdish area in the country's north, which has acted autonomously since the overthrow of Saddam Hussein's regime in the spring of 2003. If the current attempt to salvage Iraq's federal structure fails, and if the Kurdish population of Iraq starts agitating their brethren in Turkey, the latter is likely to undertake major military action to preserve its domestic security. In such a scenario, the region risks the specter of widespread instability. Among the regional powers, Iran has the greatest level of influence among various Kurdish factions and its cooperation will be indispensable to contain the negative effects of militancy.

Afghanistan. With tens of thousands of NATO troops currently stationed in Afghanistan, the necessity of containing radical Islamists there who wish to overthrow the government of Hamid Karzai is greater than ever before. In a similar vein, any attempt to contain narcotics trafficking from Afghanistan to global markets must take Iran's interests into account. Failure on this front could have a very negative effect on NATO's ability to deliver its stated objectives of greater security and development for the people of Afghanistan, who had been devastated by a generation of war, which spanned from 1979 to 2002, and which continues to fester intermittently.

Global Energy Security. As it contains 10 percent of the world's oil supplies—second only to Saudi Arabia—and 15 percent of the world's natural gas—second only to Russia—any comprehensive and long-term solution to the region's and the world's energy needs must take Iran's interests into account. Iran overlooks the strategic Strait of Hormuz in the Persian Gulf. Any large-scale instability involving Iran will have a disruptive effect on global energy markets, and the sudden rise in the price of oil may precipitate a global recession. U.S. opposition to the construction of new oil and gas pipelines through Iran has not only harmed Iran, it has set the whole region back. Iran is the most economical route for energy transportation for its northern, western, and eastern neighbors. This is especially the case with Turkey, Pakistan, Afghanistan, and Armenia. Regarding these countries, especially, U.S. policies toward Iran have been detrimental to them.

Enhancing the security of GCC countries. Iran is steadily improving relations with the members of the Gulf Cooperation Council, led by Saudi Arabia. All the GCC states remain vulnerable to radical elements who wish to disrupt their close ties to the United States. Integrating Iran into regional and international security, trade, and investment regimes will noticeably reduce the likelihood of instability among the monarchies of the Persian Gulf region.

Moderating Islamist militancy. As the country whose revolution in 1979 is universally viewed as the fountainhead of Islamist militancy in the Middle East and beyond, incorporating Iran into regional and international arrangements can send a signal to other Muslims that even the most ideological of Muslim states, and the only one in history that has had a populist Islamist revolution, can come around and be incorporated into the global economic and political system. This will have an impact that will be felt, indirectly, from Indonesia all the way to the horn of Africa, where Islamist movements have turned into potent vehicles of protest against the status quo, especially aimed at the United States.

Stemming the tide of anti-Americanism. The irony that Iran presents is that while its government has been one of the most stridently anti-American anywhere in the world, the Iranian population is, by contrast, sympathetic to the United States. Since the United States remains the world's preeminent economic, technological, and military power for the foreseeable future, its currently unprecedented unpopularity undermines the very foundations of international stability, from which no single state or group of states can benefit in the current international environment. If Iran can be convinced to drop its anti-American posture, this will send the signal to many countries that the United States has the flexibility and will power to turn its relationship around *even* with one of the most hitherto anti-American states in the world. Rolling back the current tide of anti-American sentiment—which has become endemic on all continents—will buttress the current stability of the international system, and it will make the process of reforming the deficiencies of the current order more achievable.

Enhancing Israel's security. Iran possesses the largest Jewish community in the Muslim world, and boasts a Jewish population of 30,000. By virtue of the long history—over twenty-five centuries—of Jewish presence in Iran, the country has more synagogues than any country in the region except Israel itself. Based on the historical role Iran has played in advancing interreligious harmony, Iran has the potential to spearhead regional drives to combat anti-Semitism and prejudice in all their forms.

Enhancing the viability and stability of the eight newly independent countries of the Caucasus and Central Asia. Most accounts of the dissolution of the Soviet Union agree that independence from Moscow came as an unwanted gift to the countries of the Caucasus—Azerbaijan, Armenia, Georgia—and to the countries of Central Asia—Turkmenistan, Kazakhstan, Uzbekistan, Tajikistan, and Kyrgyzstan. This was so because Russian influence had brought the notion of nationhood to these countries in the first place. However, especially with Turkmenistan, Armenia, and Azerbaijan, with whom Iran shares land borders, Iran can play a stabilizing role in cooperation with Russia and Turkey.

Enhancing the legitimacy of the United Nations system, including the International Atomic Energy Agency, and the international nonproliferation regime. Iran is currently locked in a dispute with the UN Security Council over its refusal to suspend its uranium enrichment activities. A peaceful resolution of this dispute will have a tremendously positive impact on the legitimacy of the UN, the IAEA and, more broadly, the international nonproliferation regime.

Judging by these factors, it is easy to see why Iran is a highly important country. If the current reactive vicious circle within and outside Iran can indeed be broken in favor of a proactive agenda aimed at integrating Iran into the community of nations, the benefits can be tremendous indeed.

THE PLAN OF THIS BOOK

This book takes a bird's-eye view of Iran's condition, and its current and possible future place in the international community by relying on authoritative sources and the opinions of leading experts. Part I, "Learning from the Past," examines Iranian history in the twentieth century, and explores some of the key reasons for Iran's underachievement during this time. It highlights the domestic and international factors that have stymied the country's development throughout its recent history. It emphasizes the necessity of achieving an evenhanded reading of Iranian history, which has eluded most Iranians and many outsiders to date. Part II addresses "Challenges of the Present." In separate chapters, it addresses the geopolitics of the region surrounding Iran, Iranian foreign policy, and the challenge of economic development in Iran. Part III, "Prospects for the Future," focuses on the necessity of building a "Culture of Development" in Iran by focusing on the evolving relationship between religion and state, pluralism and diversity, and women's rights in Iran. The conclusion addresses the challenge of charting a balance between independence and interdependence, and the necessity of breaking through the U.S.-Iran deadlock.

PART I

Learning from the Past

CHAPTER ONE

The Legacy of Unsustained Achievements: A Tour of Iran's Experience with the Twentieth Century

More than a century has elapsed since the constitutional revolution of 1906 in Iran, which spawned democratic institutions in a country that had been ruled by autocratic kings for many centuries. But the yearning of Iranians for building a stable, developmental order based on the rule of law still remains largely unfulfilled. Iran's constitutional revolution, the first of its kind in the Muslim world and among the first in Asia, was one of the most momentous events in the country's history as it created the country's first modern constitution and parliament, its first political parties, and laid the basis for the establishment of a modern public sphere in Iran. It would seem natural for a country that made such a significant leap toward modernization and development over a century ago to have developed into a well-functioning democracy by now, capable of meeting the moral and material needs of its people. Most indicators of development indicate, however, that Iran has not succeeded in harnessing the achievements of its past. This chapter addresses the question of why this has been so by revisiting some of the key developments in Iran throughout the twentieth century, and by delving into the extent of the hardships experienced by the Iranian people throughout that time. Any attempt to understand the contemporary Iranian national psyche must begin by considering twentieth-century Iranian history.

We aim to show that if the progressive currents aiming to develop the country throughout the twentieth century had in fact been preserved, channeled and utilized, Iran would be a far more advanced country today, and its people would enjoy a far superior moral and material condition, while boasting a superior stature in the international community. Instead of tens of thousands lining up every year to emigrate from Iran, taking their resources, hopes, and talent to countries that can utilize them, there would be an inflow of capital and talent into the country. In retrospect, the twentieth century was indeed a time of unsustained achievements for Iran. Bursts of progressive energy and periods of impressive political and economic development were not sustained, and much hard-earned productive energy was squandered. To see why this was so, we must put on clear historical lenses and, through this, we must scrutinize the main obstacles that have stymied the country's development throughout that time.

Such an attempt requires revisiting the constitutional movement of 1906–1911, which aimed to build a law-based political order in Iran; the Pahlavi era, which, in the period 1921 to 1979 advanced the economic development and modernization of the country; and the period from the revolution of 1979 to the end of the twentieth century, and, in turn, to the present, which is best characterized as an attempt at mixing religious rule as defined by the Shia clergy's idiosyncratic version of Islam on the one hand, with republicanism, based on elected offices and public representation on the other.

An open, critical inquiry into the causes of Iran's current predicament must stay clear of historical prejudice and eschew ideological blinders that have traditionally undermined genuine quests for understanding. During most of the close to six decades of the Pahlavi era, and since the revolution of 1979, which overturned it and the millennial tradition of monarchy in Iran, successive generations of Iran's political leaders have not rendered a balanced picture of the country's strengths and shortcomings. They have not produced a fair appraisal of the contributions of the people and systems they have replaced. In the postrevolutionary period's press, and especially in its public broadcasting, almost nothing has been said for over a generation about the positive contributions of the two Pahlavi Shahs, or even of Mohammad Mossadegh, the prime minister who nationalized Iran's oil. This is so despite the fact that these figures were among the most consequential and in many respects progressive political personalities of twentieth-century Iran. No monument to them, no street or institution bearing the names, can be found in the country, as though these figures never existed, except as targets of ideological derision; as though the country's history began, literally, in 1979. Such wholesale denial of history is one of the main causes of Iranians' inability to learn from the strengths and shortcomings of their past. Aristotle's advice, "know thyself," has not been heeded at the national level.

This inability to come to terms with its own national history, based on successive autocrats' attempts to wash away history and to begin, in effect, at year zero have hampered Iran's prospects at finding a balanced, sustainable place among the community of nations—akin to an amnesic adult who has little or no sense of the circumstances under which she was born, raised, and educated, and thus exhibits destructive mood swings. Ever since the revolution of 1979, which was cannily usurped by the clergy, no high government official in Iran has uttered a positive word about the Pahlavi dynasty or other Iranian kings, and, likewise, those who were affiliated with the monarchy, from self-imposed exile in the United States or Europe, have had nothing good to say about the domestic and foreign policy record of the Islamic Republic. A national rupture between the pre- and post-Khomeini eras has severed Iran's links to its past, instilling in the Iranian people an acute sense of national amnesia, which is on display in the history textbooks of the pre- and postrevolutionary periods alike.

While no nation can afford to wholly misconstrue its history, this is especially true of Iranians, whom Georg Hegel, the eminent German philosopher of the early nineteenth century, called the world's "first historical people." Referring to Iran by its classical name Persia, Hegel, in his books *The Philosophy of History* and *Aesthetics*, delved into the contributions of Iranians, from Zoroastrian times to the advent of Islam, to human progress and historical consciousness. Hegel's contemporary, Johannes Goethe, the famed poet and natural philosopher, had drawn inspiration from Hafez, the fourteenth-century mystical Persian poet, and had reflected this in his voluminous writings. Such works by leading European thinkers had in turn helped establish among the European intelligentsia the idea of the continuity of Persian civilization. In the minds of Europeans of the early nineteenth century, and more broadly, during the enlightenment, Iranians were seen as a distinct people, possessing a distinct civilization. To be sure, understanding the history of nation building in Iran requires us to go much farther back than the twentieth century.

While the first Iranian kingdom-turned empire had been established under the Achaemenid dynasty in the sixth century B.C.—and hence numerous exalted references to "Cyrus, King of Persia" in the Old Testament—the underpinnings of the modern Iranian state were laid by the Safavid dynasty, who hailed from the northern Turkic peoples of Iran. For over two hundred years beginning in the sixteenth century A.D., Safavid rulers turned Iran into one of the most powerful kingdoms of its time. During the reign of Shah Abbas the Great in the early seventeenth century, with their capital in Isfahan, Iranians made major advances in architecture, the arts, and in bringing national cohesion to their far-flung lands. The country's borders stretched at that time from Mesopotamia to the west to much of current-day Afghanistan to the east, and from the current-day territories of the Caucasus and Central Asia in the north to the shores of the Persian Gulf in the south. This was also the first time that an active diplomacy developed between Iran and the main European kingdoms, especially Portugal, Holland, and England, as well as Russia and the Ottoman Empire. In repelling the Portuguese from the Persian Gulf, Shah Abbas had received help from the English, an attempt to create a balance of power in the region which shows that strategic thinking of this sort has a four-hundred-year history in Iran.

It was upon the orders of the Safavid founder, Shah Ismail, that an official Shia sect of Islam had been adopted as Iran's state religion. This had been an attempt at distinguishing Iran from the Ottoman Sunnis, and at imbuing reigning Iranian kings with a religious legitimacy. The competition between the Safavid and Ottoman empires, more than being spurred by ethnic rivalry—since Safavid kings were Turkic themselves—was based on religious rivalry. Successive generations of Ottoman Sultans, from their castles in Constantinople, presided over a "Sultanate" and a "Khalifate," and had ruled for centuries not only as kings of a physical and geographic domain, but also as the final purveyors of Islamic truths and interpretations. The Safavid kings in Iran had similar goals, and thus throughout the two-and-half centuries of their rule, numerous wars broke out between the two

Muslim empires. For close to five centuries, before and after the Safavid period, except for brief interruptions under Shah Abbas and Nader Shah, in the seventeenth and eighteenth centuries respectively, the holiest Shia shrines of Imam Ali and Imam Hussein in Najaf and Karbala remained firmly under Ottoman control. The rebirth of the Iranian empire under Safavid kings came with the adoption of a new religion; the superimposition of religion and statecraft would in time become one of the distinguishing features of twentieth-century Iranian history.

More so than most countries, Iran has a rooted sense of national history. Yet despite the historical entrenchment of their national identity, and despite the fact that they went as far as creating a new religion to solidify this identity, Iranians are beset by an amnesia that comes from a tradition of unaccountable, despotic government that has habitually altered their history to suit its immediate political needs. Hoping to come to terms with their history Iranians have thus been forced to search in a state of darkness. This was true of the Pahlavi era; it has been especially true of the Islamic Republic. How can a people achieve steady progress if they have not been allowed by self-interested politicians to learn from their history?

* * *

Against the background of historical amnesia, Iran's development has traditionally been undermined by a multitude of internal and external factors—one having to do with the country's starting point and the domestic conditions of Iranian life at the beginning of the twentieth century and before, while the other relates to direct foreign meddling in the country's internal affairs for most of that century. Both of these factors undermined the country's autonomy and the authority of its central government, and hindered attempts at planning and institution building in Iran.

While the nineteenth century had seen rapid scientific and technological advances in Europe, the United States, and Japan, and hence their economic and political progress, the pace of modernization in Iran had been so slow that in the early years of the twentieth century the country lacked even a semblance of a modern national infrastructure: a unified standing army to keep order within and protect the country's borders, paved roads, railways, modern hospitals and schools and universities would arrive as late as the 1920s and 30s. In these areas, Iran was at least half a century, in some areas a century, behind the West and Japan. Literacy rates, throughout the twentieth century, were very low: at the time of the revolution of 1979, despite the rapid progress made in the Pahlavi era, only about half of Iran's 37 million people were literate. The corresponding figures for industrial countries at this time was well over 90 percent. Today, over three-quarters of the Iranian population are literate, a statistic that shows impressive progress in this area, but also the low baseline from which the country began.

At the beginning of the twentieth century the vast majority of Iran's 15 million people were illiterate rural dwellers, engaged in self-sustaining agriculture and animal husbandry. While the British and Russian empires had reached the zenith of their military powers at this time, and while industrialization proceeded apace in Germany, France, the United States, and Japan, Iran looked back upon the nineteenth century as a time of national disintegration. In two wars in the early nineteenth century with Russia, Iran had ceded its northern territories and, in middle of that century, defeated by Britain, it had relinquished its claim to what is now western Afghanistan. After a century of Qajar rule, Iran entered the twentieth century as a land of warring fiefdoms, its king guarded by a few thousand Russian-trained Cossacks against regional clans, its borders without meaning as foreign troops crossed them at will. A fair estimate of the level of literacy in Iran at the beginning of the twentieth century is five percent. In the developed, urbanized countries of the world, by contrast, significant majorities were already literate by this time.

Another decisive factor in the weakness of national cohesion, and a main cause of the lack of steady political and economic progress in Iran—in the nineteenth, and the first three decades of the twentieth century—was the absence of railways in the country. While most European countries and North America had built extensive rail networks on their territories by the last quarter of the nineteenth century, it would take Iran another half-century, until the late 1930s, toward the end of Reza Shah's reign, to build railways that traversed the country to connect its southern and northern ports. In the absence of rail—since Iran lacks major rivers that would enable modern shipping—the main modes of transport for Iranians throughout this time were horse- and mule-drawn carriages. This fact alone was enough to place Iran in a position of underdevelopment and utter weakness before the advances of the British and Russian empires, whose influence and power had steadily and dramatically grown in Iran throughout the nineteenth century.

Iranians lacked the know-how and technology to build the railroad themselves, and the British and Russian empires, despite having toyed with the idea in the late nineteenth century, on the whole opposed railway construction in Iran. In their opposition to the Iranian railway project, the two leading empires of the time, locked in competition over Iran and Central Asia, worried about Iranian rail falling into the rival's hands. At the same time they seem to have agreed that the building of the railway may have made Iran strong enough to resist their advances, and was thus to be avoided.

THREE PIVOTS OF IRAN'S BIPOLARITY

In at least three key areas of their national life in the twentieth century, Iranians did not succeed in creating a sustainable and progressive balance. They oscillated instead from one extreme to another. First is the relationship between them and the outside world or "foreigners," especially their relationship with the West; second is the relationship between religion and politics in Iran; and third is the makeup and orientation of political and economic elites of the country and their relationship to the masses. In each of these areas balance and sustained progress eluded Iran throughout the twentieth century as the country swung from one politically induced extreme to another, making planning and steady progress more difficult to achieve.

Throughout the Constitutional movement, and during the close to six decades of the Pahlavi era, the Iranian elite were enthralled by the achievements of Europe, America, and Russia, and they did their utmost to import their industrial, economic, and political progress into Iran. From clothing to eating habits, from standards of beauty to figures of speech, the Iranian elite saw the wholesale importing of Western artifacts and lifestyles as an all-encompassing cure for what they saw as their country's backwardness. Toward the end of the Pahlavi regime, it had even become fashionable among the well-to-do to boast that their children couldn't speak or read any Persian, and that they were more comfortable speaking English or French. And, similarly, social gatherings and evening receptions at Iran's embassies in Europe or America, featuring cocktails and tango dances, attempted to be as Western as Westerners themselves.

Then came the revolution and Iran swung the opposite extreme: a strict xenophobia set in that shunned all European and American symbols. Especially in its political leadership, Iran swung from a complete embrace of Europe and America to an unfettered rejection of them. A glance at the social habits of Iranian elites is instructive. Whereas during the reign of Mohammad Reza Shah, he and the empress and senior Iranian officials would slow dance with their European and American hosts or guests, after the revolution all Iranian government employees have been barred from even shaking hands with members of the opposite sex in official gatherings and in public life, more broadly. Unlike Iran, most countries in Asia and in the Muslim world have stayed clear of both of these extremes, giving Iran the dubious distinction of cultural confusion.

During the Pahlavi era, as the members of the royal court gradually forgot their own humble roots, the Iranian establishment was beset by an excessive elitism wherein the upper strata of society came to see themselves, in time, as being from a different country from the majority of their compatriots. They considered most Iranians traditional and thus backward. In their mannerisms and their worldview, the upper strata had little in common with the common folk, and for this reason many no longer saw themselves as Iranians. After the revolution, Iran swung to the other extreme, so much so that in the first few months after victory, revolutionary leaders would, in keeping with traditional Persian practice, sit on the floor to conduct official business, seeing chairs and tables as intruding Western imports. While looking and sounding as though they were above the people characterized Iranian leaders prior to the revolution, the opposite took hold after 1979 and an "elitophobia" set in where not only the veneer of westernization, but many aspects of technocracy and bureaucratic order, rank, and professionalism were cast aside as well.

During the Constitutional Revolution and the Pahlavi era, the Iranian state was set on reducing the power of the religious establishment in people's personal lives, in the educational system, and in the judiciary. The high point of these efforts were during the mid-1930s, when Reza Shah ordered the forcible de-veiling of women and, in a great transgression, ordered his army to shoot on protesters in Mashhad's

Gowharshad Mosque, which became ingrained in the popular imagination as a massacre in the house of prayer; thirty years later, in the early 1960s, Mohammad Reza Shah similarly ordered his army to shoot on protestors, many of them clerics, in the religious centers of Qum. As a reaction to these overt attacks on religious symbols, Iran swung to the other extreme after the revolution, as women were forcibly re-veiled this time, and the clergy took over the courts with a vengeance, ordering the executions of many thousands of political offenders in the name of religion throughout the 1980s, aiming simultaneously to export their Islamic revolution to other Muslim countries, while waging war with Saddam Hussein's Iraq, a country that was backed at that time by numerous European countries and the United States, as well as the richest Arab states—a war that ended up costing Iran dearly.

These areas of bipolarity suggest that Iran has been unable to achieve a healthy cultural and political balance. The challenge of the future is to overcome this bipolarity and to reach for the most elusive quality in modern Iranian history—sustainability. It is a well-tested truism that the two key ingredients of progress are leadership and sustainability: sparks whose energy can be harnessed and made to last in the long term. Twentieth-century Iranian history had ample examples of the first requirement, but it failed in the second. Below we shall revisit some of the most important developments in twentieth-century Iranian history to see why their achievements were not sustained. Most important, we will attempt to see what can be learned from this experience, and how Iranians can break the vicious circle of squandering their achievements.

CONSTITUTIONAL REVOLUTION

Despite the designation "revolution," which connotes sudden and often violent social and political upheaval and transformation, the beginnings of the movement to institute a constitutional, law-based system of government in Iran and the establishment of the country's first elected parliament were peaceful. In December 1905, Russia, the main foreign backer of autocratic monarchy in Iran, was itself embroiled in domestic turmoil and feeling the dejection of its defeat in the Russo-Japanese war that year. Thus, the political environment within Iran was ripe for hundreds of clergymen, bazaar merchants, and artisans to stage two sit-ins against the government. They gathered a few thousand people, first at the Shah Mosque in Tehran and two days later at the shrine of Shah Abdol-Azim in the city of Rey, twenty kilometers to Tehran's south. At the sit-ins they demanded the establishment of a House of Justice that would adjudicate their affairs independent of kingly despotism, aiming to set clear limits on the king's authority. Led by Seyed Abdollah Behbahani and Seyed Mohammad Tabatabai, two prominent clergymen, the movement simmered until it came to a head in the summer of the following year.[1]

In July 1906, aided by Behbahani's association with the British, a few thousand protesters, many of them clergymen, took refuge and staged extended sit-ins on the lush grounds of the British legation's summer quarters in northern Tehran. Since the practice of the sit-in or "bast" in mosques had been forbidden, protesters had increasingly sought refuge during this time in British, Russian, and Ottoman legations, which were not under the direct control of the Iranian government. The July 1906 sit-in in Tehran coincided with major gatherings in the mosques of Qum. The protesters demanded that the Qajar king, Mozaffar-eddin Shah, sign a constitutional order setting limits on the king's power, and establishing an elected parliament that would oversee the country's affairs, which would later include the country's foreign relations. The Shah acquiesced and on August 5 he signed the first draft, and on August 9 a more thorough decree, thus marking the birth of constitutional government in Iran. During the protests, only a few minor skirmishes had occurred between the Shah's armed guards and the protesters, and very few deaths were reported. The birth of constitutional government had come peacefully to Iran.

The first national assembly opened in October 1906; it had 156 deputies, sixty of whom were from Tehran. Half of the Tehran deputies represented the guilds, the other half were made up of merchants, landowners, the clergy, with only a handful representing the Qajar family. Whereas in the past the Qajars, with the blessing of the clergy, faced no restrictions on how they treated their subjects, now they had to officially share power with various segments of society and, by extension, with the public at large. For the country as a whole, this was a tremendous leap forward.

The main task of the first assembly was to draft a constitution that would delineate its own and the king's rights and responsibilities. An agreement emerged in the fall of 1906 that the Assembly, as the representative of the popular will, should have ultimate say over the country's laws, its budget, as well as its foreign relations. In January 1907, a week before dying, Mozaffereddin Shah signed the constitution drafted by the first Assembly.

The new king, Mohammad Ali Shah, far more despotic than his father, did not invite most Majles deputies to his coronation ceremony in early 1907, displaying the low regard in which he held their institution; this did not bode well for the future of constitutional government in Iran. Yet despite the antagonism of the new king, the Assembly pressed ahead with the attempt to reform the Iranian state. In March 1907 a committee led by Sani-al Dawla, an aristocratic deputy from Tehran, drafted a resolution that demanded a European-style system of financial administration be adopted by the Iranian government. This was to replace the system of bribes or "gifts" to the shah that had been in place until then.[2]

But, opposed to these reforms, the new Shah brought back the stern former premier, Amin-ol Soltan, to prevent a further erosion of what had been seen until then as royal prerogatives. The year 1907 was a year of political ferment in the country, especially in Tehran, as pro- and anticonstitutionalist forces, advancing in parallel, added to their ranks and solidified their demands, preparing for a seemingly imminent clash, which came in June 1908 when the Shah appointed the Russian Colonel Liakhov as the military governor of Tehran, and instructed him to bombard the Assembly's building. This caused the deaths or dispersal of many deputies and constitutional leaders. During the time of these skirmishes constitutionalists, whose supporters had taken up arms against the Cossack guards of the Shah in newly formed "associations," stood up for the rule of law and national sovereignty. Two leading constitutionalist clergymen, Malek-al-Motekalemin and Seyed Jamal Isfahani, as well as Mirza Jahangir Khan, the publisher of the progressive journal *Sur-esrafil*, and an adherent of the Shaikhi-Babi faith, were among those executed. The bombardment of the Majles and the execution of its leaders in June 1908 brought the peaceful phase of the Constitutional movement to an end. The first assembly had been convened with much hope in October 1906. Before it could finish its first two-year term, however, falling prey to an attempt to nip its democratic mandate in the bud, the Majles was dissolved. The bombardment of the Majles was part of a broader Russian-backed royal coup to bring the capital under Mohammad-Ali Shah's control.

With the Shah in control of Tehran, the core of constitutional activism and resistance moved to Tabriz, in the northwest of the country. Organized in the form of local associations or "anjomans" and helped by "Democrats" in Russian-controlled Baku, as well as Iranians of Armenian descent, tens of thousands took up arms against the royalist forces who were backed by some of the main preachers of Tabriz, and by the leading clergyman of Tehran, Sheikh Fazlollah Nuri, who had declared that constitutionalism and limiting absolute kingly authority contravened the laws of Islam. The leaders of the Tabriz constitutionalist fighters were two Iranian-Azerbaijani militia commanders, Sattar Khan and Bagher Khan, who are enshrined in Iranian memory as symbols of Iranian nationalism and progressive sentiment.

Emboldened by the hearty resistance in Tabriz, by December 1908 constitutionalists in Tehran had regrouped, with many of their leaders and a few hundred supporters taking refuge in the Ottoman legation in Tehran. In the first few months of 1909, however, Tabriz bore the brunt of the Russian-backed royalist backlash, as the city was besieged and bombarded and finally occupied by Russian forces and their domestic allies. Many thousands died during the long siege. Fearing decimation by advancing Russian regiments, the constitutional soldiers began their southward march, toward Qazvin and on to the capital, where they would be joined by revolutionaries who had risen up along the Caspian coast, especially in Rasht.

Supporting the demands of the constitutional forces, by January 1909 the southern Bakhtiari clan, led by Sardar Asad, had occupied Isfahan. By June their march had reached Qum, where they stationed a few thousand troops, waiting to march on Tehran. Finally, in July 1909, revolutionary forces comprised of Bagher Khan and Sattar Khan's troops, the northern revolutionaries from Gilan and Mazandaran, and the Bakhtiari forces from the south, orchestrated a joint march on Tehran and liberated the city. They deposed the Shah, installing his son Ahmad, a minor, as king, and hanged some of the Shah's leading supporters, including Nuri, the Shah's most vociferous supporter among the clergy. Fearing for his life, the Shah took refuge in the Russian legation in Tehran, preparing to depart the country for exile in Russia, from which he would never return.

After the conquest of the capital by nationalist and constitutionalist forces, the ground was prepared for the second national assembly to convene. It did so in November 1909 after a recess that had lasted for a year and a half, a hiatus that was a noticeable setback for the democratic momentum that had been generated by the first assembly. Upon taking shape, the new assembly relaxed the property requirement for voting, opened up elections to broader segments of the population, and ended representation on the basis of class. It also reduced Tehran's seats from sixty to fifteen, allotted nine seats for the Tabriz region, increased the representation of the provinces and provided one seat each for the Armenian, Jewish, and Zoroastrian minorities.

The second assembly also made provisions for establishing a Swedish-led gendarmerie to bring security to the countryside, as well as provisions for American advisers to establish a modern treasury tax system for the country. Among the most progressive of the assemblymen at this time was Seyed Hassan Taghizadeh,[3] the erudite and nationalist deputy from Tabriz, who led the "Democratic" faction. This faction was supported by foreign freedom fighters who were mostly from Baku and other territories to the country's north. The Democrats, derided by traditionalists who saw them as radical and irreligious, were opposed by the "Moderate" faction in the assembly, who were influenced by the views of Behbahani and Tabatabai, and by leading merchants of the Tehran Bazaar. The tension among these two factions led to the assassination of Behbahani, and led Taghizadeh to flee the country as suspicion for instigating the murder had fallen on him. Volunteers loyal to the merchants and the clergy, in retribution, targeted leading Democrats. Internal division among their ranks worked to further paralyze the constitutionalist agenda.

Throughout the term of the second assembly, while progressive and nationalist groups were nominally in control of the Iranian government, the country sank deeper into disarray and chaos. The central government was once again powerless in controlling the centrifugal forces that were unleashed across the country. Infighting among constitutional forces, as well as overt foreign, especially Russian, meddling worked to weaken their effectiveness in governing the country.

By the end of 1911, with Russian forces having occupied Rasht and Anzali, and with British forces stationed in Isfahan and Shiraz, a joint ultimatum was issued to Iran, warning against independent action by the government in general, and prohibiting the use of non-Russian and non-British foreign advisers in particular. This decree was especially directed against the American banker, Morgan Shuster, who had been chosen by the assembly and had been serving as the country's treasurer general. It aimed to protect the Russian and British rights of first refusal in the running of the country's affairs. Thus, by the end of 1911, with the national assembly dissolved once again under foreign pressure and broad internal chaos, Iran's experiment with constitutional government ground to a halt. The vast progressive potential of the constitutional revolution was thus mostly squandered. The next

Majles would not convene for another three long years. After 1911, freedom of the press as well peaceable assembly and party politics were once again severely restricted in Iran. The experiment with popular democracy, the backbone of the national revival, had been largely derailed.

The five-year constitutional movement from 1906 to 1911 marked a time of national rebirth for Iran. After steady inner erosion in the preceding century, the movement instilled a sense of modern nationalism in Iran, wherein loyalty to country took precedence over one's clan or even the figure of the king, who, up until that point, had expected absolute obedience from subjects, and had been seen as more sacred than the land and the nation, as God's shadow on earth. The constitutional movement marked the birth of a modern nation, within a very old one.

Apart from the birth of modern party politics in the country, it brought a flourishing press and, by Iranian standards of the time, a vibrant public sphere. After the declaration of constitutional government in 1906 many dozens of newspapers and journals sprouted up across the country, breathing freely after decades of Qajar-imposed restrictions on the press. For the preceding two decades, progressive political writings had been produced by Iranians in exile and sent as contraband to Iran a few hundred copies at a time. The main ones had been "Ghanun"—meaning law—which had been published in the early 1890s in London by Mirza Malkam Khan, an exiled former official and man of letters, and "Akhtar"—meaning star—which had been based in Istanbul. In the absence of local literary vehicles for democracy and responsible government, local progressives relied on Iranian sources based abroad, and on foreign sources, to keep abreast of their national affairs.

After the revolution, for the first time in their living memory, Iranians could express their views freely, and they showed how much they cherished this freedom by the waves of printed matter they produced. Newspapers and journals such as *Anjoman, Suresrafil, Mosavat, Ruh-al-Ghodos,* and *Habl-al-Matin* took on the Shah and attacked despotic government, demanding a lawful government accountable to the people. Most of the press was published by activists with secular democratic leanings and in the first two years of constitutional government the influence of the press as an agent of public education grew impressively. For the first time in the country's history, tens of thousands would read the new press across Iran, and it became customary for those who couldn't read to frequent tea houses where newspapers were read out loud.

Despite the vast potential of the new press, however, by the time of the dissolution of the second assembly in 1911, little remained of newspapers that had acted as vehicles of public education during the early years of the movement. Progressive voices were once again muted, as many of the writers, editors, and publishers of the press were killed or exiled.

* * *

The three areas of biploarity and lack of balance, mentioned above, were all at work, rendering the constitutional revolution's achievements unsustainable. On the one hand leaders of the revolution rightly fought overt foreign meddling in Iran's domestic affairs. At the same time, however, it had been contact with the outside world and foreign influences that had made the revolution possible in the first place. Initial British support for constitutionalism in Iran, and the fact that Iran's revolution was directly affected by Russia's ill-fated revolution in 1905, show that while these two empires were predominantly concerned with their imperial exploits and often worked against national progress in Iran, exposure to them had nonetheless given Iranians the knowledge and the impetus to improve their country's condition.

Interacting with kindred spirits in Russian-held territories north of Iran, who had benefited from Russian military and scientific education, and with the Britain, who was the world's most advanced and powerful empire at this time, had been a cause of progress in Iran. From the other end of the spectrum, the Anglo-Russian Treaty of 1907, which officially divided Iran into their respective spheres of influence immediately after the birth of constitutional government in Iran, was signed at a time when Iran's first assembly worked to institute laws in the country and bring order to its chaotic landscape. It is broadly accepted today that the Anglo-Russian treaty of 1907, which aimed to divide up Iran among the two empires exclusively, came as a big blow to the country's sovereignty, and to its prospects for economic and political development.

Yet it is also undeniable that nationalists, many of them devout Muslims, who charged their opponents with treason for being supplicants of foreigners, had forgotten that it was only by grasping and utilizing the knowledge of these same foreigners that progress had come to Iran in the first place. What came to be known as the hated "foreigner" in Iran's public imagination was also, especially during the constitutional revolution and the Pahlavi era, an object of overt and boundless admiration by Iranians. The love-hate relationship with the West, including Russia, which continued throughout the twentieth century, has many of its roots in the events of the constitutional revolution.

The relationship between the elites of the constitutional period with the masses in Iran was characterized by mutual distrust. In a society in which the vast majority was illiterate, in a country that lacked a modern system of education, it was indeed difficult for progressive movements to build a large national following. A small fraction of Iranians were directly involved in, or comprehended, the complexities of the evolving constitutional order. The foreign-educated elite, for their part, numbering no more than a few hundred across the country, saw the average person as ill-informed, overcome by religious superstition, and ultimately incapable of knowing their own interests. Herein lay another source of weakness among the constitutionalists: divisions within their ranks. While constitutional leaders such as Taghizadeh were social democrats with a secular, Western worldview, the revolutionary gospel was preached with the greatest impact by select members of the clergy. In time it became unclear whether constitutional leaders were more opposed to the Shah or to each other.

Throughout the constitutional period, the clergy played an ambivalent role. On the one hand they, especially Behbahani and Tabatabai, had been undisputed instigators of the revolution. At the same time, however, Nuri and other clerical proponents of the monarchy saw popular enfranchisement and setting limits on the Shah's power as contravening the laws of Islam. They were deeply suspicious, also, of attempts at importing foreign ideas into Iran. Representative government, a system of secular schools and courts, what the progressive revolutionaries sought, were deemed as undermining the authority of the clerical establishment. The ambivalent relationship between the clergy and representative, law-based government traces many of its roots to the constitutional period. On the one hand, without the clergy popularizing revolutionary sentiments in their preaching, such sentiments would have remained confined to foreign-educated elites. On the other hand, fearing their own loss of power and prestige, the clergy represented one of the most significant obstacles to building a modern state in Iran. This duality and ambivalence between religion and progressive politics would become one of the most defining characteristics of twentieth-century Iranian politics, culminating first in the success, and then in the derailment of the progressive potential of the revolution of 1979.

As we saw above, interacting with and learning from more advanced countries, especially the Russian and British empires, had been a boon for Iran's progress. At the same time, however, imperial powers also stunted Iran's development by undermining the authority of its central government and the will of its people. At no time was this more the case than during the first and second world wars, during which Iran fell prey to the advances of far superior foreign forces on its territory. Iran had tried, unsuccessfully, to remain neutral in both world wars. Yet this did not prevent imperial armies from occupying its territory and delivering punishing blows to the local population. Coming to terms with its painful past vis-à-vis the main European powers has yet to come about. This fact has undoubtedly hindered the healthy integration of Iran among the community of nations.

WORLD WAR I

By the time World War I was declared in 1914, the influence of Russia and Britain in Iran had reached a peak. In 1910 Britain had delivered an ultimatum to Iran regarding the security of southern Iran, especially the British-controlled ports in the Persian Gulf. The Russians soon followed suit and in 1911 presented their own ultimatum to Iran, which made obvious their plan to turn Iran's northern provinces into de facto extensions of Russian territory. As noted above, this forced the Iranian government to once again dissolve the parliament which, as the embodiment of popular will, had resisted foreign encroachments on the country's sovereignty.

When World War I broke out, allied forces officially occupied the northern and southern territories of Iran. In response to this development, the Ottoman Empire moved its troops into northwestern Iran to build a buffer against Russian forces. Thus, while Iran had declared its neutrality, its northern and northwestern provinces became battlegrounds for the warring parties. Officially, Russia and Britain were not at war with Iran, but, in fact, the tens of thousands of their troops inside Iran roamed the country at will and undermined the country's ability to function as a cohesive unit. In response to Russian and British designs on their country, a significant number of Iranian nationalist deputies, especially those belonging to the Democrat faction in the Iranian parliament, developed pro-German leanings. This was so because Germany, one of the most advanced countries in the world by this time, came to be seen as the only viable counterweight to the designs of imperial powers. To downgrade German influence in Iran and to solidify their hold, Russian forces began a southward march in 1915 and forced the national government to evacuate Tehran and convene in Qazvin and then Kermanshah. With the entry of Russian troops into these cities, the national government went into exile in Istanbul.

One of the most destructive policies of Russia at this time was its encouragement of ethnic rivalries in Azerbaijan by fomenting secessionist tendencies of kindred spirits in the northwestern Iranian province. This worked to uproot the remnants of the national achievements of the constitutional movement in Iran. It is noteworthy that during the constitutional movement a wide array of ethnicities, and Iran's Christian minorities—especially those of Armenian descent—had united to bring a law-based system of government to the country. One of the most damaging effects of World War I was that it significantly undermined this hard-earned unity, as well as the national cohesion and self-confidence that constitutional government had brought to Iran.[4]

One of the little known calamities of World War I and its aftermath in Iran is the widespread famine that the war engendered across the country. The most significant treatment of this subject is the book by the agricultural economist Mohammad-Gholi Majd, *The Great Famine and Genocide in Persia, 1917–1919.* Having relied on U.S. State Department archives, Majd quotes the American charge d' affaires in Persia at the time, Wallace Smith Murary, as having claimed that in 1917–1918, up to one-third of Iran's population was wiped out by famine and disease. This means that millions of people died in Iran during this time.[5]

To be sure, the exact causes of the devastating famine are difficult to grasp. Majd blames the British who, after the Russian revolution of 1917, had become the main foreign power in Iran. Having isolated farmers from their customers inside Iran the British, Majd claims, made it impossible for the country's fertile regions in its north and northwest to remain connected to the rest of the country. At the same time, according to Majd, a significant amount of the grains produced in Iran were forcibly acquired for British troops in the country and shipped abroad to other British troops in the region.

Majd concludes that, unbeknownst to most, one of the main genocides of the twentieth century occurred in Iran during and immediately after World War I. It is difficult, however, for rigorous academic research to corroborate these figures.

In addition, the word "genocide" implies the willful killing of large numbers of noncombatants. The historical record in this area is murky.[6]

Majd's work brings much-needed attention to one of the most tragic calamities suffered by Iranians in their modern history. A more extensive scholarly treatment of this subject would have to utilize "triangulation" and provide evidence from others, including British, Russian, and Ottoman sources, to show the extent of the famine and the ways in which it was affected by the war and its aftermath. In our opinion, it is essential to see the calamities that befell Iran as a product of the disruptions of war in a broader sense. Despite some of its methodological deficiencies, Majd's work is important as it helps us understand the blows that were inflicted on the Iranians' national psyche in the war years. In his more ambitious book on the impact of World War I on Iran, namely, *Persia and World War I and its Conquest by Great Britain*, Majd provides a rich account of the privations of the war. His primary focus, however, as the title implies, is once again on Britain's nefarious designs on Iran.[7]

REZA SHAH: THE SOLDIER TURNED KING

By the time Reza Khan, a colonel in the Russian-led Cossack brigade, led a few thousand of his men on horseback from Qazvin to Tehran in the winter of 1921, instigating a coup and taking over the reins of government, Iran was a country in complete disarray. The reigning Qajar king, Ahmad Shah, who had acceded to the throne in 1911 at the age of 12, and been looked after by an appointed regent, was now in his late teens and spent large portions of his time in Europe. He ruled only in name. The disintegration that had begun under his forebears had reached new heights, equating Qajar rule with impotence, despotism, and corruption in the public imagination. It seemed as though only foreign hands could keep Iran from disintegrating.[8]

In the aftermath of the Bolshevik revolution of 1917, the new Soviet government, preoccupied with solidifying the new order in Russia, had temporarily backtracked on its imperial designs on Iran. The Ottoman Empire, having been defeated by the Allies, had lost its ability to play a balancing role in Iran. Britain, by contrast, as noted above, had emerged after World War I as the preeminent foreign power in Iran, as it had occupied most of the territory to the west of Iran in Mesopotamia, an area that had been controlled for centuries by Ottoman Turks. Emboldened by Britain's newfound power in the region, the British foreign secretary, Lord Curzon, proposed an agreement in 1919 wherein Iran would become a British protectorate. After steadfast opposition from the Iranian parliament, however, Britain backtracked on this plan.

Facing stiff domestic resistance from the remnants of the constitutional movement, and unable to deal with unruly clans across the country, the British decided to back a strong central government in Iran that could bring law and order to the country by quelling the mutinies of the clans. This led General Edmund Ironside, who commanded British forces in northern Iran, to consult with a colonel in the

Cossack Brigade who had established a reputation among his men as a resolute man of action. Reza Khan was told by Ironside that he would have Britain's backing if he mobilized his troops and marched on Tehran. Since Britain was by far the strongest foreign power in Iran at this time, Reza Khan took Ironside's promises of cooperation to heart.

For the next two decades until 1941, when he was deposed and exiled by British and Soviet troops that occupied the country during World War II, Reza Khan (who crowned himself in 1925 and thus became Reza Shah and adopted the name "Pahlavi") transformed Iran from a woefully underdeveloped country plagued by widespread chaos to one that had, by the time of his departure, had the infrastructure and institutions of a modern nation. The twenty years of Reza Shah's rule were thus a time of national integration and renewal for Iran, making him the most important figure of the twentieth-century history of the country. Yet his reign, especially its latter half, also came with rising despotism and corruption, a common trait of unaccountable systems of government.

During his reign Reza Shah became the most powerful king Iran had seen in over a century and a half, harkening back to the time of Nader Shah and Karim Khan Zand, who had brought national cohesion to the country and expanded Iran's regional and international influence in the mid-eighteenth century. But despite this distinction, Reza Shah died in exile in South Africa in 1944, while his son, Mohammad Reza, reigned as the new king in Iran. This humiliation for Iranians was compounded by the fact that it took seven years after his death for Reza Shah's corpse to be brought back to Iran. After the revolution of 1979 his mausoleum was demolished by the revolutionary government, marking a high point of the country's politically induced amnesia. No official memorial or tribute remains to this day of the father of modern Iran. The same is true of the second Pahlavi king, Mohammad Reza Shah.

Born in 1878, and descending from a line of military men, Reza Khan had joined the Cossacks in his late teens. The Cossack forces, the most advanced fighting units that Iran possessed at this time, had taken after similar formations in Russia, and had been created in Iran in the 1880s at Nasser-eddin Shah's behest, to serve under the command of Russian officers, in exchange for concessions to Russian tsars. In this sense, Russia directly helped lay the foundations of the modern military in Iran. Reza Khan had served for two decades under the command of Russian officers. Having been born in the northern village of Savad Kuh, Reza Khan had grown up in Tehran and had begun his service in the barracks as an infantryman. Since it was customary at this time for Cossack units to guard foreign embassies and banks, early in his career, coinciding with the opening years of the twentieth century, Reza Khan was stationed as a guard in front of British, American, Dutch, German, and Russian embassies, and other official and business establishments.

Beginning in 1903, Reza Khan, then in his twenties, took part in numerous military campaigns against mutinous clans across the country, in support of the central government in Tehran. During the campaign at Shahabad, his boldness in battle won him promotion to third lieutenant. In 1911 he was a leading member of the force that put down the rebellion of the Kalhur clan in Hamadan. He was involved in similar pursuits in the northwestern town of Ardabil. It was also in 1911 that he was promoted to second lieutenant and placed in charge of a leading machine gun unit. In 1912, having excelled in his duties, he was promoted to lieutenant. Around this time, in his late twenties and into his thirties, he led his men in battle in the regions of Kurdistan, Luristan, and Khorasan, among others. He was distinguished and revered by his men for his frontline service in these campaigns. By 1916 Reza Khan had been promoted to lieutenant colonel and had been stationed in Russian-led infantry units in the north-western cities of Kermanshah and Hamadan. The following year he was called to Tehran and placed in charge of one of the Cossack regiments, only to be sent again to Hamadan to train an army unit in that city.

Over his two decades of service in the Cossacks, before instigating the coup of 1921, Reza Khan had become personally acquainted with the far-flung corners of Iran. He had spent only brief periods in the capital during this time, remaining mostly on active duty and traveling on horseback throughout the troubled provinces. In this way he had developed an intimate familiarity with Iran's rugged terrain, and with the peculiarities of its diverse peoples. For two decades he had seen, firsthand, the challenge of bringing order and uniformity to a chaotic land where loyalty to clan, and sometimes foreign masters, took precedence over national duty. Having risen through the ranks of the army and having been shaped in his formative years by its culture, he resorted often to the physical punishment of infractors, and he habitually used harsh language to make his point. Feared by his subordinates as excessively demanding, he was simultaneously revered by his men for his bravery in battle and the dedication and patriotism he brought to his duties. His image as an intrepid man of action had been buttressed by his physical appearance, his pressed uniform and shiny boots, and his tall and burly physique and piercing eyes. He struck fear in people's hearts, but also gave them hope for a better future, a way out of nationwide chaos and disintegration.

As he followed events during and after the constitutional movement, Reza Khan was incensed at the power of foreign forces in Iran, and at Iranians' weakness. While the Cossacks, in whose ranks he had served all of his adult life, worked to bring badly needed order to the country, they did so only at the behest of their Russian masters. At the same time, beginning in 1915, the British had begun training their own local army, the South Persia Rifles, to protect their trade routes in Iran's south. The gendarmerie, as noted above, was led by Swedish officers. As a nationalist he conceded the foreigners' superior power and lamented Iran's relative backwardness, but he also hoped to one day build a national army led and operated by Iranians themselves. This was indeed one of the main accomplishments of his rule. One of the most influential newspapers he read was *Raad*—meaning thunder—which was published by Seyed Zia-eddin Tabatabaie, an erudite, cosmopolitan anglophile and a nationalist who bemoaned the power of foreigners in Iran and the country's inability to stand on its own feet. It was Seyed Zia, well known by this time in political circles in the capital, who served Reza Khan as co-conspirator during the 1921 coup. He became prime minister after the takeover of Tehran, while Reza Khan became the war minister. True to his temperament, Reza Khan soon deposed Seyed Zia and entrenched himself as the ultimate power broker in Tehran.

In the first four years of his de facto rule, before crowning himself as king, Reza Khan, as war minister and later as premier, initiated major reforms in the country, which he continued throughout his sixteen years as king. While the constitutional revolution had laid the foundations of modern Iran, especially in making provisions for a system of national education and secular courts, it was Reza Shah who put these ideas into practice across Iran, building the physical infrastructure that allowed these advances to be institutionalized. In that sense, he pushed forward many of the ideals of the constitutional revolution and was a major force for the progress of the nation. These efforts, especially the attempt to institute a modern educational system and judiciary, were mostly opposed by the clergy, and this caused a steady deterioration of his relationship with the religious establishment.

Reza Khan's most important achievement in the first two years after the coup was establishing order across the country. Within a year of the coup of 1921, his troops quelled the disturbances of Iran's south-central Fars province, the rebellions of northwestern provinces of Kurdistan and Azerbaijan, as well as the mutinies in the northern provinces of Mazandaran and Gilan, and in the northeastern province of Khorasan.

In 1921 Reza Khan also founded a unified, uniformed, and nationwide army in Iran, dissolving the Russian-led Cossack brigade. In that year he dissolved the Swedish-led gendarmerie, which was in charge of internal security. In a bold act that undoubtedly buttressed his nationalist credentials, Reza Khan expelled all foreign officers from the army, making it open only to Iranian nationals. Having made male conscription mandatory, within a decade after his coup Reza Shah had built a modern army in the country, its troop numbers surpassing 100,000, its ranks drawn from across the country, transcending ethnic or clan or family origins. In this sense especially, the new army was the key institutional agent of nation building and modernization in Iran. Reza Shah himself sent all of his five sons to the military academy, and required that they always appear in uniform in public functions. Following his lead, it became customary throughout his reign for leading families to send their children to military school and then to the military academy. Two of the most significant military families that this tradition produced were the Minbashians and the Jahanbanis, two successive generations of whom served under Reza Shah and his son, making important contributions to the country's modernization and progress.

Within a year after the coup, Reza Khan's troops quelled disturbances in Tabriz. He began a nationwide project for paved road construction. In 1924, he annulled aristocratic titles and instituted a national registrar, and established the modern practice of adopting last names, and instituted a nationwide system of conscription for the army. Having led the annulment of the Qajar dynasty in Iran, and impressed by Ataturk's establishment of a Republic in Turkey the year before, he seriously entertained the idea of declaring a republic in Iran, and becoming the country's first president. But faced with stiff opposition from the clergy, especially from Seyed Hassan Modarress, who feared that similar to the clergy in Turkey they too would be stripped of their social role and privileges, Reza Shah opted for continuing the monarchical tradition in Iran.

As his years as war minister and premier gave way to his time as king, Reza Shah worked on reducing foreign influence in Iran. In 1927 he annulled most foreign oil concessions, especially to the British, only to be forced in 1933 to reinstate them. In that year Davar also created the bases for Iran's modern judiciary system. In 1928 he founded the National Bank of Iran, which replaced the British-controlled Imperial Bank of Iran.

In 1934, he founded the University of Tehran, the country's first university, and inaugurated the Agricultural Bank of Iran, ordered the de-veiling of women, and instituted the country's first labor laws. In 1938, under Swedish and German supervision, the national railway project, ten years in the making, was complete and connected the Persian Gulf to the Caspian coast. The completion of the Trans-Iranian Railway Project was one of the most significant achievements of Reza Shah's reign. The railway project was funded almost exclusively by locally levied taxes on tea and sugar. It is unlikely that a less resolute leader could have brought the project to fruition.

While his ethic of hard work and self-reliance and discipline, and his dogged determination to build modern institutions in Iran served Reza Shah and the nation well, his increasing despotism and corruption, which intensified in the second half of his reign, mar his legacy. Throughout the 1930s Reza Shah confiscated for himself many hundreds of hectares of prime land across the country, becoming the country's biggest landlord. At the same time, he grew increasingly jealous of the influence of capable and educated men whose talents he had utilized and learned from during his modernization drive. Two such key personalities were Abdol-Hossein Teimurtash (his minister of court during the first seven years of his reign [1925–1933]), and Ali Akbar Davar (1885–1937), who as minister of justice under Reza Shah in the late 1920s founded he new judicial system in the country. He also created the country's first census bureau, and along with Teimurtash, led the creation of a modern bureaucracy in the country.[9]

Teimurtash, the son of a major landowner in the Khorasan province, had been sent as a teenager to St. Petersburg to be educated in tsarist Russia's military academy. There, as was customary among the Russian elite, he had also become fluent in French. Upon returning to Iran in his twenties, Teimurtash honed his elocution skills in Persian and became one of the most prominent deputies of the national assembly. Davar, similarly, had been educated in Europe and learned about the dominant ideas in law and international relations.

Teimurtash and Davar had also been among the key founders of the Tajadod—meaning modernization—Party in Iran in the mid-1920s. This party, wedded to modern and secular ideas, had lobbied hard in the assembly and prepared the ground for Reza Shah's accession to the throne. Teimurtash, in particular, a charismatic, educated member of the elite, provided the intellectual backbone for the creation of the new dynasty. Himself far less privileged in background than Teimurtash, and far less worldly, Reza Shah used his services astutely, and rewarded him with the post of court minister. Throughout his seven-year tenure as court minister, Teimurtash served as Reza Shah's alter ego and his chief propagandist. He also took over much of the portfolio of the foreign minister and led Iran's negotiations with Britain over oil concessions. Yet throughout this time Reza Shah had been growing increasingly jealous of Teimurtash's rising power and popularity. Suspecting, in addition, that he had grown close to the Soviet Union, in 1933 Reza Shah ordered him arrested and killed in prison. With this act and many like it that followed, Reza Shah eroded his hard-earned legitimacy. None of the Shah's men felt secure in their positions, and many, for good reason, lived in fear while serving in senior posts. A similar fate befell Davar as well. Having turned against him, Reza Shah publicly humiliated him, and drove him to suicide after a wrenching period in which Davar feared for his life. In the army, the pillar of Reza Shah's rule, there was a similar insecurity. Sardar Asad Bakhtiari, one of the leaders of the constitutional revolution, was first given the portfolio of war minister, only to fall into disfavor with the Shah and be killed on his orders. Reza Shah was also jealous of his top army brass and hindered leadership development in the army, lest the top officers build power bases on their own.

Davar's achievements were similarly impressive. With a background in journalism and law, he was not only the founder of a modern judiciary system in Iran, but also the originator of numerous state-led enterprises in the country. In his mid-twenties, having graduated in the humanities from Iran's only institution of higher education at this time, the Dar-al Fonun, he wrote prolifically in Iranian newspapers, especially focusing on the challenges of modernization confronting the country. In his late twenties he left for Switzerland to pursue a doctorate in law at the University of Geneva. After Reza Khan's coup d' etat, he returned to Iran and became the director general of the newly founded ministry of education. Soon after this he entered national politics and was elected to parliament as a deputy. Working closely with Teimurtash in the Majles, he was instrumental in paving the way for the creation of the Pahlavi dynasty, which was made possible by abolishing the previous Qajar dynasty.

Once Reza Khan became king, Davar was entrusted with founding Iran's Ministry of Public Utilities and Trade. From this position he also oversaw the beginnings of the planning for the Iranian railway project. On the judicial front, while the foundations of modern judiciary in Iran had been laid in Iran during the constitutional revolution, it was Davar who put incipient ideas of a modern judiciary into practice. In the late 1920s, under his supervision, the Majles passed scores of pieces of legislation including a civil code, a criminal code, and a commercial code. During his seven years as minister of justice, Davar founded hundreds of new courts across Iran and selected and trained capable judges. In the 1930s, for over five years, Davar served as the minister of finance, and laid the foundations of modern trade practices between Iran and other countries. As noted above, despite his achievements, Davar committed suicide as he felt his prominence had aroused Reza Shah's envy and feared for his life in his final months.

His ill treatment of his top advisers, especially Teimurtash and Davar, without whom he would arguably not have acceded to the throne in the first place, mar Reza Shah's legacy. Partly, this shortcoming in Reza Shah was attributable to his modest level of literacy and shallow understanding of international affairs. Despite this, however, Reza Shah must be counted as the father of modern Iran, and the most consequential figure in the country's twentieth-century history.

WORLD WAR II

When World War II broke out, Iran declared its neutrality, as it had done in the previous world war. Yet this declaration did not allay British and Soviet anxieties of Iran falling under Germany's control. Britain had demanded that Iran expel the few thousand Germans who worked in Iran as advisers. Reza Shah had rejected this demand, considering it a foreign intrusion into Iran's affairs. Thus, three months after Germany invaded the Soviet Union, British and Soviet forces invaded Iran in full force on August 25, 1941. Soviet troops invaded from the north and northwest, while British forces came in from Iran's western border, from what is current-day Iraq, and from the Persian Gulf in the south.[10]

Facing the onslaught of far superior forces, the Iranian armed forces, numbering over a hundred thousand by this time and built painstakingly over the previous two decades, unraveled. The Iranian navy in the Persian Gulf, led by Rear Admiral Gholam-Ali Bayandor, who had been appointed as the military commander of the key ports of Abadan and Khorramshahr, was decimated in a flash. Bayandor was among the hundreds of Iranian naval officers who were killed in battle. Iran's land forces put up a fight initially, but after Reza Shah's orders to cease hostilities they abandoned their barracks to avoid a similar decimation. The sting of humiliation, once again, crept into the country's collective consciousness. Close to forty years later, in the 1980s, the dammed up humiliation of past defeats burst forth in the eight-year war with Iraq as hundreds of thousands of Iranians volunteered and showed great heroism in defending the country against foreign aggression.

The invasion and occupation of Iran, which lasted five years during World War II and its aftermath, fundamentally undermined the country's inner cohesion, and degraded the authority of its central government. The presence of foreign troops fanned xenophobic sentiments. The disruption wrought by the occupation, especially acute in rural areas, forced the migration of hundreds of thousands into the cities, which made the country even more unstable. While under foreign occupation, the Soviet Union and the United States competed over oil concessions in the country. In December 1945, after the war had ended, the Soviet-allied Azerbaijan Democratic Party, led by Jaafar Pishevari and guided by a pro-Soviet ideology, declared autonomy. At the same time, secessionists in Iran's western province of Kurdistan proclaimed independence and established the Kurdish Republic of Mahabad. Both of the secessionist parties enjoyed direct support from the Soviets, and received protection from Soviet troops that continued to remain in large numbers in Iran's northern and northeastern provinces. After the war, while the American and British forces left Iran as they had promised, Soviet troops did not.

Through the wily diplomacy of Prime Minister Ahmad Ghavam, better known as Ghavam-ol-Saltaneh, who was one of the most accomplished politicians of the Qajar and Pahlavi periods, the Soviets were offered oil concessions, and through American and British pressure, Stalin was finally persuaded to respect Iran's territorial integrity. To further placate the Soviets, Ghavam chose three members of the pro-communist Tudeh party for his cabinet. Ghavam was later able to rescind his concessions to the Soviets, by relying on strong public opposition to the move. In December 1946, Ghavam sent the Iranian army into Azarbaijan and brought the province back into the national fold. In the absence of Soviet support, once his government unraveled, Pishevari fled to Moscow. Similarly, the Kurdish Republic of Mahabad came apart. When the new parliament convened in 1947, the National Front, led by Mohammad Mossadegh, overwhelmingly defeated the Soviet oil concessions. The parliament also ratified a bill that forbade the granting of new concessions, and required the government to exploit oil resources directly. This was a precursor to the nationalization of Iran's oil, which was led to fruition by Mossadegh during his premiership in 1952.

MOHAMMAD REZA SHAH: THE COSMOPOLITAN

When viewed together, the Pahlavi father and son's reign brought rapid advancement and modernization to Iran. The period 1921–1979 was on the whole a time of profound transformation for the country. For at least half of this period, however, the political freedoms of speech and assembly were severely restricted, and Iran's political development was thus significantly set back. Stifling the public sphere and the press, in turn, fed the power of the religious establishment, since it was only in the mosques that people could gather to voice their dissent. This caused both Pahlavis to work steadily, sometimes using force, to reduce the influence of the clergy in Iran, despite the fact that the majority of the population held strong religious beliefs and counted on the clergy for social and spiritual guidance.[11]

Mohammad Reza Shah was twenty-one years old when he acceded to the throne in the summer of 1941, after the allied invasion and occupation of Iran that had deposed his father and sent him on a British ship into exile in South Africa. Having been installed on the throne by foreign occupiers and living throughout his thirty-seven-year reign with the fact that his country was under foreign occupation in the first five years of his rule, Mohammad Reza Shah, similar to his father, developed an ambivalent attitude toward foreigners. He revered them as he owed them his throne and because he looked up to their culture and progress, and he simultaneously detested them for trampling on Iran's independence and territorial integrity. This love-hate relationship with foreigners was one of the main areas of similarity between father and son.

As their respective reigns advanced and their power was solidified, father and son both focused on building an independent role for Iran in international relations, and thus laid the foundations of the country's modern foreign policy. During their reign, tens of thousands of Iranians joined the ranks of Iran's burgeoning bureaucratic and diplomatic corps, and became capable and well-informed representatives of Iran in international forums.

In their personality traits, to be sure, father and son were different. The second Pahlavi, having grown up in privilege, was sent to boarding school in Switzerland. During his youth he gained fluency in French and English, becoming the first king of Iran to reach that distinction. Throughout his reign he was an avid reader of the world press and was viewed as one of the best-informed leaders in the Middle East. This was one of the reasons the Shah became OPEC's leading price hawk in the 1970s, guiding, along with King Faisal of Saudi Arabia, quadrupling the price of oil in 1973. The Shah's unbending determination to keep oil prices high in the 1970s had been a cause of concern to European countries, and even to the United States, his main ally. This picture is on display in the memoirs of former French president Valery Giscard d'Estaing in which he recalls raising his concerns about high oil prices with the Shah. In a similar vein, a long essay on the Shah in *Time Magazine* of November 4, 1974, was entitled "Oil, Grandeur and a Challenge to the West."[12] The following passages in the *Time* essay are especially telling:

At the Treasury Department, for instance, the Shah is generally thought of as a tyrant and a megalomaniac whose stubbornness and greed over oil prices represent a threat to the economic stability of the world. Treasury Secretary William Simon has publicly described the Shah as a "nut" and as "irresponsible and reckless."

What makes the Shah a key figure in the Middle East, some U.S. diplomats believe, is the fact that like Secretary of State Kissinger, he has managed to deal equably with both sides. He considers the Israelis arrogant and even "masochistic." But Iran nevertheless provides Israel with 50% of its oil. In return, Israeli experts on irrigation and land reclamation have transformed Iran's Ghazvin Plain into a fertile oasis. At the same time, the Shah responded favorably last October (1974) to a request from Saudi Arabia's King Faisal and dispatched six Iranian air force C-130 transports to ferry Saudi troops and equipment to the war against Israel. High on the agenda of Kissinger's talks with the Shah will be the unresolved confrontation between their two governments over rising oil and commodity prices.

The Shah, whose government will spend $1 billion this year to subsidize imports of meat, wheat, sugar, and soybeans, insists that rising oil prices are no different than rising commodity prices. He seeks to tie the two together in an economic index that would help to limit further increases. The U.S. position is that oil is artificially priced, which the Shah himself admits, while agricultural increases are a response to free market conditions. President Ford, and Kissinger in his latest United Nations speech, abruptly cautioned the oil-producing nations not to price their product at disastrously high levels. The Shah, more accustomed to hand kissing than hard words, bristled. "Nobody can dictate to us," he told newsmen on a state visit to Australia and New Zealand. "Nobody can wave a finger at us because we will wave back." In his 90-minute interview with TIME, . . . the Shah warned, "If this is a serious policy of the U.S. Government, then on this subject we are going to have a very serious clash."

Unlike his father, who left behind little autobiographical accounts of his life, Mohammad Reza Shah published four books during his life that outline his worldview.[13] Reza Shah's formative years had been marked, in contrast to his son's, by the harsh realities of survival as an Iranian officer in a foreign-dominated army, and later by front-line service in Iran's turbulent zones. Mohammad Reza Shah would make up for his lack of military experience by becoming a capable jet and commercial pilot—the first leader of a developing country to have done so—as he test-flew generations of military aircraft imported into Iran during his reign, well captured in his last years as king by pictures of him in the cockpits of the American-made fighter jets. Mohammad Reza Shah became a debonair cosmopolitan leader who took ski trips to St Moritz, while his father had remained, despite the wealth he had amassed, a soldier in his mannerisms and conduct.

The most substantive book published by the Shah was his first one: *Mission for My Country*. Over 300 pages long, it appeared in 1961, when the Shah was forty years old. It was written in close consultation with Dr. Donald Wilhelm, Jr., an American academic who worked as a visiting professor of political science at the University of Tehran, whom the Shah called "a personal friend and a friend of my country" in the preface to the book.[14]

In the chapter on "My Father and His Revolution," the Shah pays homage to his father, and discusses the chaos and helplessness that pervaded Iran before Reza Shah's takeover in the early 1920s. He discusses Reza Shah's breakthroughs and his creation of modern institutions in Iran.[15] It is interesting, however, that the Shah voiced misgivings about his father as well. This is how the Shah concluded the chapter on his father:

> It must be remembered, too, that my father possessed a very different personality from mine. His nature admirably qualified him for the task he had to perform, but it would have been ill-suited to the demands of today . . . As I shall presently show, my father was himself part of the environment that powerfully molded me. But even that strong influence could not make us alike. If I had been born when he was (perhaps as his twin brother) and had lived under identical conditions, I feel sure that our personalities would still have been different. My father's inborn characteristics served his country better then but, notwithstanding my admiration for him, I think that mine are of greater service to it now.[16]

This passage shows some of the origins of the Shah's insecurity, which would continue throughout his reign. According to Abbas Milani, the author of the definitive upcoming biography, the Shah had mixed feelings toward his father, whom he saw as overshadowing his own legacy. This is evident in the fact that during his thirty-seven-year reign very little was written about the life and legacy of Reza Shah; indeed, it is ironic that the two most significant biographies of Reza Shah in Persian were published in the late 1990s, during Mohammad Khatami's presidency. This is partial proof that the Shah had misgivings toward his father. The feeling was probably mutual, as it is probable that Reza Shah did not see in his first son the attributes of steadfastness and resoluteness that he would have deemed as essential in making a successful ruler.[17]

The most important chapter in *Mission for My Country* is titled "My Positive Nationalism." Here the Shah lays out in detail the necessity for Iran to develop mutually beneficial relations with *all* countries in the world. While he bemoans the negative effects of "imperialism," especially concerning Great Britain and the Soviet Union, he is careful to mention the positive relations that had developed between Iran and these countries during the Pahlavi dynasty. The Shah distinguished his "positive" vision from Mossadegh's negative and, in the Shah's view, reactionary approach to Iran's relations with imperial powers.

There is nothing more dangerous for a man or for a nation to be a prisoner of one's personal sentiments and a captive of one's egoism. After all, I had more plausible personal grounds than Mossadegh for being angry with the British. Had they not been instrumental in getting rid of my father? Had they not helped welcome the Russians into my country during the Second World War? While Mossadegh stewed in his emotions, I tried to think of the larger national interest. I have already explained that Mossadegh's negative nationalism not only provided the communists with their ideal opportunity but, paradoxically, allowed the British more influence over Iran's national policies than even before. . . . Certainly one lesson we have learned is that those who preach negative nationalism are automatically suspect. Anyone can tear down; fewer can build up.[18]

Twenty years after his first book, the Shah published his last book as a homeless former king who was shunned by the United States and Europeans whom he had seen as Iran's primary allies. He searched in vain for a home in which to spend the last days of his life. Of the world's eminent statesmen, only former president Richard Nixon joined President Anwar Sadat of Egypt at the Shah's funeral, which was held in Cairo after his death there on July 27, 1980.

In *Answer to History* the Shah refers to the sources of his disappointment at the United States. "This kind of shifting, double-minded policy I would encounter often in exile. It had mired my last months in Iran when I never knew from one day to the next what U.S. policy was, or how reliable it was."[19] While obviously embittered and crushed by his exile, the Shah dedicated a large part of his last book to the achievements that his reign had brought to Iran.

Once again, the most important section was the chapter on foreign policy. The Shah outlined the achievements of his reign in this area and discussed the mutually beneficial ties that Iran had built across the international community, while focusing on Iran's neighbors. He reserved his most lavish praise for Turkey.

"Since my father's time," he wrote, "Turkey and Iran have been faithful friends. For Iran, the prosperity and greatness of Turkey were of fundamental importance. Today I fervently pray for the happiness of this valiant people."[20] Simultaneously, the Shah recounted his positive relations with Saudi Arabia: "As a faithful Muslim and Defender of the Faith, I hope that Saudi Arabia will always remain the guardian of these holy places, Mecca and Medina, where millions of pilgrims travel every year on the path to God."[21] Similarly, the Shah recounted the progress he had achieved in expanding Iran's ties with significant powers such as China and India.

In defending his policy of building Iran's armed forces, the Shah wrote:

> Our military projects were never kept secret. Quite the contrary, they were well known to all. President Carter had reiterated his support for our endeavors at our meetings in Tehran in December 1977, when he had called our nation an "island of stability" in a very troubled part of the world. Iran was truly the only nation capable of maintaining peace and stability in the Mideast. My departure has changed all that. The Soviet invasion of Afghanistan and the terrorist attack in Mecca demonstrate this all too well.[22]

The eminent American journal, *Foreign Affairs*, published an unflattering review of the Shah's last book. It wrote, "The late Shah's thoughts, as he spent the last period of his life in exile and isolation, make a bitter and pathetic testament. Americans who have made their judgment on him and his place in history are unlikely to change their minds through reading this self-serving and superficial book . . . " Looking at the history of the Middle East since the Shah's departure from Iran, and the unprecedented violence and instability that the region has witnessed in this period, it would be fairer to claim that history has actually vindicated the Shah's views on Iran's foreign policy and the significance of its place in the international community.[23]

Despite their differences in personality and erudition, the Pahlavi father and son had a great deal in common. Similar to his father, Mohammad Reza Shah was a nationalist who wished to advance Iran's position domestically and in relation to other countries. Similar to his father, as noted above, he was installed as king with overt foreign help, was reinstalled through a foreign-led coup, and died in exile. And building on the precedent set by his father he attempted to balance foreign powers against one another; during his reign Iran established diplomatic relations with all major powers, including India, the Soviet Union and China.

Similar to his father Mohammad Reza Shah had an ambivalent relationship with his own elites. On the one hand he nurtured excellence in government and administration in the army and the bureaucracy, and trained highly capable leaders. On the other hand, insecure in his own position, he undermined his subordinates and forced them out of decision-making roles.

This can be said about the relationship between the Shah and some of the most progressive and capable leaders during his reign: Ahmad Ghavam, Abolhassan Ebtehaj, Hassan Arsanjani, four-star generals Fereidun Jam and Fatollah Minbashian, and others like them, especially Mohammad Mossadegh, were sidelined precisely because of their pioneering and progressive achievements. Arsanjani's major achievement had been his service as agriculture minister for two years (1961–1963), during which time he had formulated and implemented a land reform program that ended the lingering traditions of feudalism in Iran. Having been centrally involved in Iranian politics in the preceding two decades as a writer and strategist for nationalist causes, Arsanjani was dismissed from his post as minister and sent to serve as Iran's ambassador to Italy. Upon his return in the late 1960s, he was sidelined from national politics at the Shah's behest.[24]

The Shah did not tolerate prominence among his subordinates and thus while he had helped build leadership potential in the cadres, he worked simultaneously to undermine it by micromanaging even the smallest aspects of policymaking. In his thirty-seven-year reign the country had thirty-two prime ministers. In this sense, he severely hampered the development of leadership in the country. This quality was especially evident in the last few years of his reign leading up to the revolution. It must be said in his defense, however, that while he did exclude, exile, and imprison the political elite, unlike his father, he did not kill them.

One of the greatest tragedies of the second Pahlavi Shah's reign is the treatment he meted out to Dr. Mohammad Mossadegh, who is broadly viewed as one of the most significant political personalities of twentieth-century Iran, with impeccable nationalist credentials. Mossadegh had been active in national politics as a parliamentarian since the 1920s. His career culminated in his two-year tenure as prime minister from 1951 to 1953, during which time he led the nationalization of the country's oil. This was the main reason—the other being a real fear of communist expansionism in Iran—that the American- and British-backed coup, code-named "Operation Ajax" toppled the popularly elected Mossadegh in August 1953. In the face of a popular uprising led by Mossadegh, the Shah had fled Iran, reluctant to return. Mossadegh had nationalized Iranian oil the year before and in so doing had become a hero to most Iranians. After the coup that restored the Shah to the throne, Mossadegh was imprisoned for three years, and lived afterward for over ten years under house arrest, until his death in 1967. With Mossadegh's government out of power, the Shah reinstated the oil concessions to the major western oil companies, known as the "Seven Sisters." As he owed his throne to foreigners, he looked to them for direction in matters of governance for the rest his reign. There are indisputable signs that he had lost the will to govern as the winds of revolution swept across Iran in 1978–1979. In response to this current, the Shah sought the advice of American and British ambassadors in Iran—over and above his own civilian and military advisers.

One of the greatest tragedies wrought by the coup was the incarceration and execution of Dr. Hossein Fatemi (1917–1954) who had served as Iran's foreign minister and deputy prime minister under Mossadegh. Fatemi came from a religious family that was active in the realm of letters. He was educated in law in Tehran and Paris. He had published his nationalist ideas in his own newspaper, *Bakhtar-e Emrooz*, which means "Today's West," and elsewhere. He had started his newspaper writing and pamphleteering in his early twenties. For over a decade, he had supported the cause of national sovereignty and criticized the corruption of the Pahlavi court and their ties to imperial powers. After Fatemi's execution in 1954, a year after the coup, Mossadegh credited him with having been the instigator of the country's oil nationalization drive.

According to Stephen Kinzer's book, *All the Shah's Men*,[25] which is the most comprehensive account of the coup of 1953, it was that coup that prepared the ground for the revolution of 1979, and its anti-American focus, which Iran also tried to export to the rest of the region. The coup was carried out by Royalist Iranian army officers, under the direction of the CIA and the MI6. It tainted the image of the imperial army as being a pawn of foreigners, especially the United States. Most of the historiography on the coup has correctly outlined its negative effects. Secretary of State Madeleine Albright acknowledged this in a historic speech delivered in Washington, DC, on March 17, 2000. She said,

> In 1953 the United States played a significant role in orchestrating the overthrow of Iran's popular Prime Minister, Mohammed Massadegh. The Eisenhower Administration believed its actions were justified for strategic reasons; but the coup was clearly a setback for Iran's political development. And it is easy to see now why many Iranians continue to resent this intervention by America in their internal affairs.[26]

While acknowledging the historic nature of Albright's apology, it is also necessary to judge the coup in the context of the time in which it occurred. It is widely known that with Stalin in power in the Soviet Union in the early 1950s, the Cold War had reached a peak. As we saw above, Iran had been under foreign occupation for five years in the previous decade. Especially pertinent to this discussion is the fact that the Soviets had shown their imperial designs on Iran by refusing to end their occupation of the country's northwestern provinces in 1946. Given the rising strength of the pro-Soviet and communist Tudeh Party in the early 1950s, the lingering secessionist sentiments in the provinces, and the fact that most of the army remained loyal to the Pahlavi order, it is by no means clear that Iran could have managed to maintain its territorial integrity under a Mossadegh-led government. This period in Iranian history could well be one in which the demands of democracy and the demands of territorial integrity were at loggerheads.

A decade after the coup, in 1963, the Shah acquiesced to American demands and signed a "capitulation" order that immunized the thousands of American military advisers in Iran from prosecution in Iranian courts. This, in turn, provided fodder to Seyed Ruhollah Khomeini, who buttressed his own nationalist credentials by openly attacking the Shah for selling the country off to the Americans. This led to Khoemeini's exile for fourteen years until February 2, 1979, when he returned triumphantly to adoring masses who felt liberated from foreign domination by the revolution he had led.

Immediately after his return from exile, which was one week before the revolution's final victory, Khomeini was taken to the Behesht-e-Zahra cemetery in the south of Tehran, where he addressed tens of thousands of adoring followers. He ended his speech by addressing the armed forces:

> I want to advise the military . . . that we want you to be independent . . . Mr. General, Mr. Major General, don't you want to be independent? Do you want to be servants [of foreigners]? I advise you, join the people and say what the people say. Say we have to be independent. The people say the military has to be independent. Our military shouldn't be servants of American military advisers and [other] foreigners . . . I thank those officers who have joined the people and counsel those who haven't to do so. Islam is better for you than heresy, the people are better for you than foreigners. Do not think that if we come [to power] we will hang you . . . We want a system of the people in the service of the people, not a system led by others [foreigners].

PILLARS OF NATION BUILDING AND REGIONAL STABILITY

Similar to his father, the Shah saw a strong military not only as protection against foreign and domestic threats, but also as an agent of modern nation building. Indeed the armed forces were the cornerstone of the Pahlavi order as they brought a uniform shape to the country's personnel landscape. The new army, navy, and air force also held up Iran's position as a pillar of stability and peace in its region. The national conscription that Reza Shah instituted brought millions of Iranians into uniform and in the case of many from rural areas became an agent of literacy, Persian language acquisition, and a general sense of belonging to the nation, above and beyond their ties to clan and ethnic origin. Indeed if the Pahlavi order is to be seen as a time of major progress in Iran, its men and women in uniform must be seen as one of the main enablers of this progress.

Toward the end of the Pahlavi era, the Iranian armed forces enlisted hundreds of thousands of men in the army, and tens of thousands in the navy and air force. These forces were led by officers who were graduates of the Iranian military academy, which had been instituted under Reza Shah. Three of the significant operations of the Iranian armed forces that contributed to regional stability and maintained Iran's dominant position were "Amma," in 1969–1970; the Iranian military's leadership in containing the rebellion in Oman's Dhoffar region in 1973; and a military presence inside Iraq during operation "Ararat" in 1974–1975.

Upon Saddam Hussein's accession to the de facto leadership of Iraq in 1969, the Iraqi government, backed by the Soviet Union, issued repeated warnings to Iran to respect Iraq's exclusive sovereignty over the Shat-al Arab, the river that separates the two countries. The Shah responded defiantly by seeking for Iran navigation rights extending to the midway line of the river. Once the war of words escalated in 1969, Iraq issued an ultimatum to Iran that its ships would be targeted if they dared to enter the waterway without Iraqi permission. In response to this provocation, the Shah initiated operation "Amma" by dispatching Navy Captain Ramzi Ataaie to navigate his large gunboat named Ibn Sina into the Shat-al Arab or Arvandrood in Persian. The Iranian artillery divisions in western Iran and the

Iranian air force were instructed to provide cover. Seeing Iranian military power as superior, Iraq desisted from following through on its threats.

While war didn't break out between Iran and Iraq in the early- and mid-1970s, relations between them remained tense. During this time, Iranian forces provided intelligence and logistical support for Molla Mostafa Barzani's Kurdish guerillas, who had been locked in conflict with Iraqi forces in the previous decade. In 1974, as the climate of suspicion between the two countries continued, Iran stepped up its military support for Kurdish insurgents inside Iraq by initiating operation Ararat. Led by the artillery division stationed in the city of Rezaiye in northwestern Iran, which was commanded by the then Major General Jaafar Sanei, Iran sent numerous artillery regiments into Iraqi territory.[27]

Covered by artillery and air force units that bombarded Iraqi positions from inside Iran, the Iranian units entered Iraq through the Tamarchin pass in the Kurdish border area, and advanced about fifty kilometers into Iraqi territory. Iranian special forces remained inside Iraq for more than four months and kept up the pressure. Operation Ararat was a tool utilized by the Shah to pressure Saddam Hussein into sharing the Shat-al Arab river with Iran. It was successful as Iraq finally backtracked on its exclusionary demands. It helped compel Saddam Hussein to agree to meet with the Shah in Algeria in March 1975, and to sign the Algiers Accord with Iran in which Iraq recognized Iran's claims for sharing the waterway. The Algiers accord also committed Iraq to ceasing its claims over Iranian territory in the oil-rich Khuzestan province in Iran's southwest. Iran, in response, agreed to cease supporting Kurdish insurgents inside Iraq and to evacuate all its troops from Iraqi territory. Molla Barzani and his closest aides were given refuge inside Iran after the accords.

Another example of the Iranian military acting as an anchor of regional stability was demonstrated in the role it played in 1973 in containing the communist-backed rebellion in the Dhofar region of southern Oman, which had been simmering since the mid-1960s. Seeing the rebellion as a threat to the status quo across the whole Persian Gulf region, the Shah dispatched numerous regiments from the regular army and special forces to support the Omani government in its battle with the separatist insurgents. The rebellion was fully defeated by 1975. In his book, *Answer to History*, the Shah wrote:

> In 1973, at the request of the Sultanate of Oman, I provided this state with military aid. Oman was then threatened by the Zofaris, who were supported by Southern Yemen, the communists, and the Chinese. Our troops in Oman intervened in a vigorous way until the Sultan, who is my friend, succeeded in dominating the situation . . . China retired from this conflict after establishing diplomatic relations with Iran.[28]

Domestically, too, as mentioned above, the Iranian military played a crucial role in stabilizing Iran and countering irredentist local tendencies. In the early 1960s, for example, the army was dispatched to contain the rebellious Ghashghaie clan that sought autonomy from the central government. Intermittent operations continued in Iranian Kurdistan throughout the 1960s and 1970s.

One of the distinguishing features of many among the Iranian military's top brass during the Shah's reign, and one of the reasons they were successful agents of development across the country, was that they were knowledgeable about Iran and the world at the same time. Their knowledge about Iran came from years of active duty across the country, and from interacting with all strata of society and people of different ethnicities that made up Iran. Their knowledge of the world was attributable to the education many received at the foreign military academies of Britain, France, Russia, and the United States, during which Iranian officers became familiar with the military advances of their time. To elucidate this point, we will provide a brief biographical account of three of the most impressive Iranian generals during the Shah's reign: air force General Mohammad Khatami, and four-star army generals Fatollah Minbashian and Fereidun Jam.

General Mohammad Khatami—not be confused with the reformist cleric of the same name who was the president of Iran in 1997–2005—was born in 1919 in the northern city of Rasht. He attended the American College of Tehran, which was later named Alborz Collegiate. He then attended the Iranian military academy in Tehran, and continued his military education in Germany, Britain, and the United States. Khatami is considered to be the father of the modern Iranian air force, and Iran's first jet pilot. His flying skills had so impressed the Shah that he chose Khatami as his personal pilot and his special adjutant. In 1958, before his fortieth birthday, Khatami had ascended to the rank of brigadier general in the newly founded Iranian air force and was chosen by the Shah as its commander. The following year he married the Shah's sister Fatemeh Pahlavi. He was a founding member of the Royal Acrojet Team. For seventeen years, until his death, he remained at the helm of the Iranian air force and transformed it into one of the most powerful in the region. He developed close ties with his American counterparts who supplied Iran with the most advanced military equipment throughout his command. Khatami was revered by his men as a highly astute and knowledgeable officer whose love of flying extended to hang gliding. It was this hobby that precipitated his demise. He died in a hang gliding accident in the late summer of 1975. With his death, Iran lost one of the most distinguished officers it had produced in the Pahlavi era.[29]

General Fereidun Jam came from a distinguished Azerbaijani Iranian family and was born in 1915. His father, Mahmoud, had served as a leading politican in both Pahlavis' reign and also as prime minister under the second Pahlavi. Jam completed his high school education in France, and then his military training at Saint-Cyr, France's premier officer training institution. He also underwent training at the British and American military academies. In his mid-twenties he returned to Iran and began active duty in the army. He rose rapidly through the ranks and was appointed as the commandant of the Iranian military academy and immediately after promoted to brigadier general. In 1969 Jam became the chairman of the joint chiefs of the Iranian military. In 1971, however, the Shah, who had grown jealous of Jam's popularity, sent him into retirement, replacing him with the far less efficacious General Gholamreza Azhari, who had a reputation for being weak-willed and a mere puppet of the Shah. After retiring him from the army, the Shah appointed Jam as Iran's ambassador to Spain. In that position, too, he served with distinction by becoming semifluent in Spanish in a short time. Jam moved to London in the 1970s. As of this writing, he still lives there and is in his early nineties.[30]

General Fatollah Minbasian came from a military family. His father had been the founder of the tradition of marching bands in the Iranian army under Reza Shah. He was born in 1919, and attended Iran's military academy with the Shah, graduating with him in 1939. In 1953, in his mid-thirties, Minbashian was promoted to brigadier general. As a major general he was appointed as the commander of the army in Fars province. As a lieutenant general he became the commander of the third army corps. In 1970, still possessing the vigor of youth, he became the commander of the Iranian army, and was promoted to full general. Having been educated at the Command and General Staff College of the U.S. Army in Fort Leavenworth, Kansas, Minbashian also served as the commander of Iran's military academy for a while. He was a highly voluble and charismatic leader, fluent in English and French, and an accomplished violinist. Unfortunately, however, similar to Jam, the Shah saw him as too independent-minded and outspoken. Less than a year after being placed at the helm of the Iranian army, the Shah sent him into retirement. Prior to the revolution of 1979, Minbashian left for France, where he died in the summer of 2007.[31]

An important book published in Tehran in 2003 sheds light on the thinking of the Shah's top generals about his strengths and shortcomings. Based on the writings and interviews of generals Jam and Minbashian, the book provides a deep look at the Shah's insecurity toward military men of distinction. An unwillingness to delegate responsibility, even to his most ardent followers, was the Shah's main shortcoming. As these top generals' accounts make clear, the Shah became progressively convinced that he had to supervise even the smallest aspects of military and civilian policymaking. This was especially true in the last decade of his rule leading up to the revolution of 1979.[32]

It is indeed undeniable that one of the Shah's key weaknesses was his abiding envy toward eminence in others, even among his military's top brass, who constituted the backbone of his regime. It is documented in the memoirs of his chief confidante, court minister Assadollah Alam (quoted by Babaie), and in the above-noted book by Motazed, that the main reason for the early retirement of Jam and Minbashian was that these men were professional army officers who did not see themselves as the Shah's puppets, and who felt that the Shah should not micromanage all aspects of military policymaking. Being vocal advocates of their views and their steadfast commitments to their jobs placed them at loggerheads with the Shah. To be sure, it is to the credit of the Pahlavi order that it trained such men in the first place. It was undoubtedly a main shortcoming of the Shah, however, and a sign of his deep personal insecurity, that he feared eminence and professionalism among his subordinates. It is worthy of note that none of the Shah's generals who remained in their posts, such as generals Gholamreza Azhari, Abbas Gharabaghi and Azizollah Zarghami, was in the same league as the above-noted officers who received early retirement. Nowhere was this more true than in the elite Royal Guard, most of whose men were turned into personal servants of the Shah—at odds with their mission as professional officers. This, undoubtedly, played a role in the military top brass's declaration of neutrality immediately before the revolution's victory.

Continuing the direction set by his father, Mohammad Reza Shah successfully pushed the economic and cultural modernization of Iran. With the inflow of tens of billions of petrodollars into the country, Iran's annual income in the last decade of the Shah's rule had quadrupled and the living standards of Iranians grew so rapidly that those trends, if sustained into the 1980s, would have made Iran's per capita income rival South Korea's or Spain's. Today, after a quarter century of Islamic government, Iran's per capita income is half of what it was in the last years of the Pahlavi era.

Another key shortcoming of the Shah was that he severely restricted political activity, disallowing political parties from flourishing, and stifling the press. For two to three years in the early 1960s, at the behest of the Kennedy administration, the Shah had granted more democratic freedoms. But soon he had reverted to his dictatorial ways. One of the reasons his reign unraveled so quickly was that the Shah, having made himself the source of all decision making in Iran, could not rely on others to bring the brewing chaos under control. Suffering from what he knew was terminal cancer, the Shah, lost the will to govern in the last two years of his reign. As he fell apart, so did the Pahlavi order as no one beneath him knew what to do in his absence. For a decade prior to his downfall, he had not allowed his army commanders to meet in his absence, lest they develop a power center on their own, independent of him. Similar to his father, the Shah died in exile. It is undeniable, in hindsight, that the fifty-seven years of the Pahlavi dynasty, though burdened with shortcomings, was one of the most productive periods in modern Iranian history. Unfortunately for the two Pahlavi Shahs and for Iran, Reza Shah knew too little about the outside world, while his son, well versed in foreign affairs, possessed insufficient knowledge of Iran's domestic condition.

THE DECADE OF REVOLUTION AND WAR

The end of the Pahlavi monarchy in Iran in February 1979 completely undermined the regional balance of power. Soon after achieving victory, revolutionary courts led by Sadegh Khalkhali, a cleric, who worked at Khomeini's behest, began executing dozens of top military officers and the Shah's ministers. Soon after victory, Khalkhali's courts summarily executed some of the most distinguished among Iran's military leaders: Major General Manuchehr Khosrowdad, the head of army aviation, who commanded Iran's burgeoning squadrons of advanced helicopters, air force Lieutenant General Nader Jahanbani, one of the key leaders of the modern Iranian air force, and many of their colleagues who had been exemplary officers with unblemished records, were among those executed. Among the civilian ranks, similarly, foreign minister Abbas-Ali Khalatbari, who hailed from one of Iran's most distinguished families, and former prime minister Amir-Abbas Hoveyda, both of whom practiced the highest levels of ethics and erudition, were put before firing squads.

Within a year after its victory, the direction of the Iranian revolution of February 1979 transformed not only the country's system of government, but also its foreign policy. While the overhaul of the form of government in Iran and ending its millennial kingly tradition was foreordained by the victory of the revolution, the radical and violent direction that Iranian foreign policy took was not. The revolution had been only eight months old, and in its formative stages, when mobs overran the U.S. embassy in Tehran and took its staff hostage. Blinded by their zeal, they probably did not realize that by climbing the walls of the U.S. embassy they had hijacked the revolution itself and set the direction of the country's foreign policy for a decade. The Iraqi invasion of Iran in September 1980, as the hostage crisis dragged on, solidified the radicalism of the revolution, and this in turn defined Iran's foreign policy for the remainder of the decade.

Seyed Ruhollah Khomeini, the revolution's leader, had not supported hostage taking as an instrument of policy. However, upon realizing the gathering avalanche of popular support for the act, and confronted with a fait accompli, he had joined the radical mood that the act had ignited in the national psyche. The revolution had come to power relatively peacefully, with around two thousand deaths, as the Shah had refused to order broad bloodshed against his countrymen and women. The hostage crisis unleashed, indirectly, a decade-long wave of internal and external violence on a large scale, a classic case of unintended consequences typical of revolutions.

The eight-year war with Iraq, the bloodiest war in Iranian history and the most economically destructive, became the most important influence on Iranian foreign policy throughout most of the 1980s, a decade in which, energized by that war and its regional fallout, terms such as "terrorism," "suicide bombing," and "Islamic revolution" worked their way into the lexicon of international relations across the globe. Enraptured by Khomeini's charisma and their own religious zeal in the 1980s, untold thousands of young Iranians engaged in "martyrdom operations" and went willingly to their deaths, spurred by instilled hopes of ascending to heaven upon leaving the earthly domain. Hundreds of thousands of Iranians lost their lives, many more were maimed, and the country suffered hundreds of billions of dollars of economic damage before the clerical leadership realized the need for a fundamental change of course. When cease-fire was finally declared in the late summer of 1988, Iran and Iraq recognized each other's prewar borders. It would become the war that both sides lost. While Iraq was supported by all of the world's major powers, who sold it advanced weapons—including chemical weapons—to be used against Iran, and while Iraq was financially backed by the richest of the Arab monarchs in the Persian Gulf region, Iran fought the war alone. This was the main reason that the toll of the war's dead and maimed fell disproportionately on Iran.

With the end of the war with Iraq and with Khomeini's passing the following year, reality finally set in. Iranian revolutionaries who had wished to export their creed came to realize, painfully, the limits of Iran's influence over the Muslim world. Iran's radicalism had turned not only the United States, but most of the Arab world, Turkey, and many other countries against it. Iranians had been engaged, after all, in a devastating war with a fellow Muslim country, home to the holiest shrines of the Shia faith. The revolutionaries had repeatedly declared during the war that "the path to Jerusalem passes through Karbala." Little did they know then that Iran, despite expending much blood and treasure, would not even manage to capture Basra, which lay immediately beyond Iran's border, inside Iraq. The bitter reality that no amount of religious zeal could overcome Iran's economic and technological underdevelopment turned the mood of zealous elation into dejection, and the revolutionaries' religious idealism into a geopolitical realism.

The end of the Iran-Iraq war and Khomeini's passing meant the revolutionary phase in Iranian foreign policy had run its course. Under the two-term presidencies of Ali Akbar Hashemi Rafsanjani and Seyed Mohammad Khatami (1989–2005), as Seyed Ali Khamenei served as the country's supreme leader, Iranian foreign policy gradually overcame the vestiges of the decade of revolution and war and reverted, albeit implicitly, to the prerevolutionary foreign policy that had focused on protecting Iran's national interests through building regional and international partnerships, and a geopolitical vision based on the tested idea of building a balance of power among foreign countries, with trade and investment ties that were mutually beneficial for Iran and its partners. Moving beyond the Islamic and revolutionary excesses that had placed Iran at loggerheads with much of the world, the emerging foreign policy focused on reaching a symbiosis not just with Iraq, but also with Arab countries that had supported it, and beyond.

During the 1980s, the term "national interest" could not be found in any document or declaration relating to Iranian foreign policy. This picture changed steadily after Khomeini and by the mid-1990s, during Rafsanjani's second term in office, a national interest-based and cool-headed foreign policy was instilled in Iran, resting on realpolitik calculations. Despite lingering revolutionary slogans that have aimed to attest to the contrary, this reversion of Iranian foreign policy to a national interest orientation has continued to the present day and shows no signs of abating. Those who had thought that the revolution had permanently changed Iran's foreign policy had already been proven wrong by the mid-1990s. What Mohammad Reza Shah had termed his "positive nationalism" was reinvoked, based on the goal of establishing working relations with all the major powers. As it turned out, the revolutionary transformation of Iranian foreign policy was a short-lived phenomenon. In Rafsanjani's second term and during Khatami's presidency, a foreign policy discourse was institutionalized in Iran, in the country's press, magazines, and foreign policy journals, which, in all but name, harkened back to the Pahlavi era.

THE ISLAMIC REVOLUTION'S REPORT CARD

Throughout the postrevolution period, clerics who have come to rule Iran have condemned the violence and brutality of the Pahlavi regime, as have many foreign observers, while discussing the violence perpetrated by the Shah's secret police and the imperial armed forces against the Iranian people. Yet, in retrospect, and by comparison, it is now clear that the Pahlavi order valued the sanctity of human life far more than the revolutionary order that replaced it. This is evident in the relatively small number of political executions in the fifty-year Pahlavi reign, during which time hundreds of people had been given the death penalty for political offences. And during the revolution itself, despite the fact that mutinous demonstrators had attacked police and army units—with millions of people in the streets, and tens of thousands of army personnel dispatched to maintain order in urban centers—less than two thousand people died. Thus, resorting to extreme violence was not a characteristic of the Pahlavi regime. The revolution changed that. In the first decade of clerical rule, tens of thousands of people had been executed for political offences, most of them belonging to leftist groups. To be fair, violence was also perpetrated by leftist-Islamist groups, especially the Mojahedin Khalq organization; the ensuing armed insurrection of these groups was perhaps the leading cause of the brutal government crackdowns. In the first few months after the revolution's victory, newspapers published pictures of the executed bodies of the Shah's military and other leaders. This was attributable, in part, to the unraveling of the social fabric, and to the zeal with which revolutionaries had taken over the government.

The rule of clerics represented the first time in modern history when the national identity of Iranians was suppressed and denied. To be sure, during the two-term presidencies of Rafsanjani and Khatami this changed somewhat, judging by their pronouncements about the sanctity of Iran and the national interest. Yet if this can be said about a few members of the clergy, it has not been the case among most of them. Sadegh Khalkhali shamelessly demolished Reza Shah's tomb, planned to do the same to Persepolis, and slaughtered thousands of perceived and actual political opponents in the name of religion.

In another campaign against Iranian history, in Isfahan, the shining example of Persian architecture, all references to Shah Abbas, who had built the city's monuments in the late sixteenth and early seventeenth centuries, were erased and replaced by religious names. The "Shah's Square" was renamed "Imam Square," even though no Imam had ever had anything to do with the building of these monuments. Hotel Shah Abbas was renamed Hotel Abbasi. The most egregious assault on the Iranian people's national identity was the transformation of the Iranian flag. The clergy erased the symbol of Iranian nationhood, the lion and the sun, which had adorned Iran's flag since the Ghaznavid period 1,000 years ago. While successive kings from various dynasties were also guilty of attempting to erase history, the clerics' attempt to begin at year zero in 1979 belongs to another category.

Despite these setbacks, Iran has also progressed in the postrevolutionary period. Literacy has advanced steadily in the countryside, and women's participation in the running of the country has steadily risen as half of all university seats are now occupied by women. On the whole, the eight-year war with Iraq was economically and psychologically disastrous for the country as the clergy chose to drag it on until 1988, despite Iraq's offer of peace and reparation in 1982. Only after hundreds of thousands of Iranians were killed or maimed in those eight years, and after hundreds of billions of dollars of economic damage to Iran did Khomeini choose to "drink the cup of poison" and acquiesce to an end in hostilities. At the same time, however, the war mobilized millions of Iranians across the country for a common purpose, the largest mass mobilization of its kind in Iranian history. In this sense, it left a positive effect on nation building as diverse strata, young and old, urban and rural, pulled together to defend the country against a foreign aggressor. On the one hand, the war took a major toll on Iranian lives and the country's economy. On the other, it showed the capacity of self-reliance amongst Iranians and imbued their country, which had been overrun by foreigners throughout the twentieth century, with a new-found confidence. In that sense, more than being a religious venture, the war was based on Iranians' sense of nationalism, an experssion of their zeal as they rushed to the frontlines to defend their homeland.

* * *

The three areas of bipolarity outlined at the beginning of this section have been all working in the post-revolutionary period as well. In the first area, in its relationship with foreigners in general and the West in particular, Iran has been overtaken by a virulent xenophobia after the revolution in which Europe and the United States, far from being seen as harbingers of progress, have become objects of overt ideological derision by a government that has ruled, if only in slogans, in the name of justice and revolutionary liberation. Terms such as "global arrogance" have been devised to refer to European countries and the United States. While it is possible to argue that Iran had gotten too close to the West, especially to the United States, compromising its independence and national integrity, it is equally true now that postrevolutionary ideological blinders have taken Iran to another extreme. Viewed in retrospect, neither of these extremes have been positive for Iran's development and healthy integration into the community of nations.

As a sign of the continuing ire that Iranian leaders have drawn across the world, President Mahmoud Ahmadinejad's statement in late October 2005 that Israel be "wiped off the map," has been condemned by all major countries, and by a joint resolution of the United Nations Security Council. Ahmadinejad's speeches, including the one he delivered at the UN General Assembly in September 2005, are replete with references to the Hidden Shia Imam, whose apocalyptic return is supposed to bring order and justice to the world. Iran is the only country in the world whose leaders have such dubious distinctions, and thus it has no choice but to change its ways if it wishes to embark upon development and a peaceful symbiosis with other countries, especially with Europe and the United States.

In the relationship between elites and the masses, too, Iran has swung from one extreme to another. While an excessive elitism had driven a wedge between Iranian leaders of the Pahlavi era and the public at large, the postrevolutionary period has witnessed a turning away from the educated classes as education and worldliness have been seen as corrupting foreign influences. Throughout the past quarter century millions of Iranians, many of them possessing world-class credentials, have fled Iran for countries where their talents can be put to use. Since the revolution the yardsticks for selecting people to the country's leadership positions in all branches of government have revolved around an ideological commitment to religious and clerical rule. The capable bureaucratic and technocratic elites that were nurtured under the six decades of Pahlavi rule at great expense to the public treasury, have been supplanted by undereducated strata whose shallow knowledge of international affairs and Iran's position in it has left a great deal to be desired.

Viewed from the outside, Iran may well appear as suffering from a cultural schizophrenia. In October 1971, celebrating the 2,500th anniversary of the founding of the Persian Empire, the Shah and the Empress hosted dozens of world leaders in Persepolis in south-central Iran, with the ostentatious festivities and hospitality rivaling anything that could be found at the time in European high society. Less than a decade later, in a cultural and political about-face, Iranian revolutionaries climbed the walls of the American embassy in Iran, taking its staff hostage, instigating an unprecedented international crisis and placing Iran in a state of international disrepute, from which it has yet to extricate itself. Was this the same Iran that had been called an "island of stability" by President Carter during his state visit to Iran coinciding with the 1977–1978 New Year's celebration? In less than a year after that visit, Iran was in the midst of revolutionary turmoil, and the same country that had acted as America's staunchest ally in the Middle East and served as an anchor of the region's security was on the way to becoming, as far as the United States and its European allies were concerned, one of the most active sponsors of international terrorism, and one of the main threats to regional stability.

While in the Pahlavi Era there had been an attempt at a forced separation of religion and the clergy from public life, after the revolution Iran swung to the other extreme as the clergy forced their way into positions of power in the country's universities, its courts, as well as its police and armed forces. In meting out death sentences to thousands of people, they charged them with "heresy" or working "against the will of God" or "spreading corruption on earth." In the Iranian and international imagination these acts have been ingrained as attempts at taking Iran back to the middle ages. This point has been especially driven home by the fact that, charged with moral crimes, dozens of people have been stoned to death in Iran in public spectacles since the revolution. Similar numbers have been hanged publicly, their corpses paraded around cities, dangling from construction cranes. Iran seems to have reverted indeed to a dark age. How can a democratic, legitimate, and developmental order be built, many continue to ask, when the clergy, having taken over the government by force, rule in the name of God and charge their opponents with apostasy for political convenience? How can effective national public policies be crafted when the clergy rule in the name of Islam and as leaders of all Muslim peoples, when Iran has no authority or capacity to decide how life is to be lived in the vast majority of Muslim countries whose leaders do not share the Iranian clergy's retrograde religiosity?

The answers to such questions suggest that to develop and join the ranks of forward-looking nations, Iranians have no choice but to fundamentally reappraise the legacy of the past quarter century, and to institute reforms that can balance the religious and ideological underpinnings of the clergy's power with democratic processes that meet the legitimate expectations of the international community in the early twenty-first century. These are questions that will be taken up in the rest of this book.

PART II

Challenges of the Present

CHAPTER TWO

Between East and West: The Geopolitics of Iran

On April 11, 2006, in the holy city of Mashhad, Gholamreza Aghazadeh, director of Iran's Atomic Energy Organization, stood boldly before the world's TV cameras to make an announcement. With traces of an Azeri accent adorning his Persian speech, in the presence of President Ahmadinejad and top military officials, and carried live by CNN and other major broadcasters, Aghazadeh declared that Iran had successfully enriched uranium using domestically developed technologies. He said Iran's decision to enrich uranium at will was irreversible and that since such advances were made possible by domestic talent and initiative, Iran was confident in its ability to use nuclear energy for peaceful domestic purposes. President Ahmadinejad, too, has become the champion of Iran's right to have access to nuclear energy. His steadfast defense of Iran's rights in this area has won him noticeable popularity within Iran and among other developing countries.

While Iran's current leadership cannot publicly admit this, the pride and credit they have taken in Iran's progress in nuclear research were made possible by Mohammad Reza Shah's policies three decades before. The Shah had laid the foundations of the country's nuclear program in the 1960s and 1970s, at a time when Iran was seen by the Nixon and Ford administrations and America's European allies as the lynchpin of stability in the Persian Gulf and, along with Turkey, a first line of defense against communist expansionism in a vitally important part of the world. Developing Iran's oil and gas reserves, the pursuit of alternative energy sources, and the drive for regional prominence had been the hallmarks of the Shah's foreign policy, held up by the special relationship Iran had at the time with the United States. As early as 1957, during the Eisenhower administration, Iran had signed an "Atoms for Peace Agreement" with the United States. A decade later, in 1967, the Shah's government signed a contract with AMF, an American company, which led to the building of the Nuclear Research Center in Tehran. In the mid-1970s, Iran signed major contracts with French, German, and American companies to build a dozen nuclear reactors across the country.[1] With each passing year, the foreign policy of the Islamic Republic in the post-Khomeini period, beginning in the early 1990s and extending to the present, has increasingly come to resemble that of the Shah. Yet Iran needs more political maturity before its leaders can overcome their denial of history and admit the debt they owe to the government their revolutionary comrades overthrew. Learning from its own history is indispensable for Iran, if it is to succeed in building a healthy and sustainable relationship with major players on the world stage, especially with the United States and its allies.

One of the key slogans of the millions of demonstrators who took to the streets during the revolution of 1978–1979 was "Neither East, nor West, an Islamic Republic." This chapter aims to show that contrary to this slogan, Iranian foreign policy would be far more productive if it were anchored in current and historical reality, and based on who Iranians are and where their country is located: a cultural, economic, and geopolitical bridge between east and west. That is the main challenge and the greatest promise of Iranian foreign policy in the years ahead. To achieve this, Iranians must fully digest, and overcome, the reactionary aspects and the rigidly ideological underpinnings of the revolution of 1979. Iran needs to promote its interests while serving the cause of regional and international stability, not as a real or perceived source of rebellion and tension. Only then can Iran transcend the reactionary aspects of its foreign policy in favor of a proactive and productive vision based on peaceful coexistence with its neighbors and the international community at large.

THE ORIGINS OF MODERN FOREIGN POLICY THINKING IN IRAN

The origins of Iran's modern foreign policy and the corresponding strategic vision and "balance of power" thinking trace their roots to the Safavid dynasty in the early sixteenth century. As we saw, Safavid kings hailed from the northern Turkic peoples of Iran. Since the Persian Shahs and the Ottoman Sultans ruled at this time as custodians of the Islamic faith, with the founding of the Shia faith as Iran's state religion at the outset of the Safavid dynasty in the sixteenth century, the two main Muslim empires of their time became embroiled in numerous wars with one another. These wars were based on religious competition and the fact that neither side recognized the legitimacy of the other's religious beliefs. For close to half of the fifty-two-year reign of Shah Tahmasb, the second Safavid king, in what is known as the period of the "twenty-year wars," numerous bloody battles broke out between the Persian and Ottoman empires, during which Tabriz, the Safavid capital, and many towns in eastern Anatolia and the Caucasus were repeatedly captured, ransacked, and recaptured by the two sides. It is an ironic testament to deep bonds between the two sides that during much of this the "Persian" Safavids used their native Turkish language to communicate with their Ottoman compeititors, while the Ottoman "Turks" used Persian as the official language of their court in Constantinople for a few centuries.[2]

In his quest to bring unity to Iran's armed forces, Shah Abbas benefited from the advice of two English envoys, Anthony and Robert Shirely.[3] Sent to Qazvin to propose British help in containing the Ottomans, the Shirley brothers gained the Shah's trust and enabled him to develop a better grasp of international affairs. This contact with the English also enabled Shah Abbas to introduce, for the first time, modern military practices, including artillery regiments in Iran. Based on Anthony Shirley's advice, it was in 1599 that, for the first time, the Shah dispatched his envoys to European capitals to gain their support in his plans against the Ottomans, with whom numerous European powers shared borders, and with whom they had been engaged in many wars. Emboldened by assurances of support from Austrians and Hungarians, in 1602 Shah Abbas invaded Ottoman forces in Tabriz and took back the city. In the first decade of the seventeenth century, Shah Abbas, in a series of military victories made possible by his refurbished army, took back all the territories in Western Iran and the Caucasus. To distance it from the Ottomans, Shah Abbas moved his capital to Isfahan in central Iran, where he would commission the building of some of the most marvelous monuments that remain the pride of Iranian architecture to this day.

In another defining achievement of his reign, Shah Abbas used his ties to England to pressure the Portuguese to end their occupation of numerous Persian Gulf islands and to abandon their naval encirclement of Iran in the south. By the time of his death in 1629, Shah Abbas had institutionalized a system of governance across the vast expanse of his empire. This cohesion outlasted him for a full century. During his reign Iran established diplomatic relations with all of world's major powers, east and west. He can thus be seen as the father of Iranian foreign policy in the modern sense of the term.

After the dissolution of the Safavid dynasty in the early eighteenth century, Iran began a period of decline. No dynasty managed to bring a lasting cohesion to national life until the rise of the Pahlavi dynasty in the early twentieth century. To be sure, Iran had instituted a balance-of-power policy during the four-year premiership of Mirza Taghi Khan Amir Kabir, who in the late 1840s and early 1850s, had brought order, cohesion, and professionalism to Iranian foreign policy, which had suffered under the corruption and impotence of Qajar rulers. Amir Kabir's murder at the hands of Nasser-eddin Shah's henchmen, however, worked to nullify many of Amir Kabir's attempts at domestic and foreign policy reform. After Amir Kabir, it would take Reza Shah's ambition to bring back national integration to what had once been a mighty empire.

FOREIGN POLICY IN THE PAHLAVI ERA

Under the two Pahlavi shahs (1925–1979), Iran built a modern foreign policy bureaucracy with staffed embassies in dozens of countries across the world. It was at this time that Iran attempted to actually implement the balance-of-power foreign policy backed by a modern infrastructure, modern and well-equipped armed forces that protected the country's borders, and a gendarmerie that brought security to the countryside. While the revolutionary zeal of the 1980s attempted to undo the balance-of-power achievements of the Pahlavi era, it largely failed in that effort. The most significant challenge confronting Iranian foreign policy in the Pahlavi era was maintaining national cohesion when Iran, in economic, technological, and military terms, had little ability to defend its interests in the international arena.[4]

During World War II, as we saw previously, the Soviet Union and Great Britain invaded Iran and occupied it in less than a month. The new shah began his reign when his country was under occupation, and lived with this bitter fact for the next five years. During the famous Tehran Conference, which convened on November 25–28, 1943, where Roosevelt, Churchill and Stalin had gathered to strategize on ways of winning the war and dividing up the world afterwards, the Shah was not even invited as an observer to any of the allied leaders' discussions. The Iranian authorities had not been notified that the allied leaders had chosen their capital as one of the two the most consequential Allied summits during the war. Even the diplomatic nicety of acknowledging the Shah as the host was not observed. In the minds of the participants, it seemed, Iran was not a country at all, but a mere playground for their imperial designs. To send a clear signal as to who was in charge in Iran, Soviet and British troops were moved to the center of Tehran on the very day that the second Pahlavi shah was sworn into office in the late summer of 1941.

The same logic was at work when a CIA- and MI6-backed coup overthrew Prime Minister Mossadegh's government in 1953, and restored a reluctant Shah to the throne. For most of the twelve years he had been on the throne before fleeing the country in 1953, the Shah had not felt in command of the country as major powers dictated many aspects of Iran's destiny. For half this time, Iran had been under foreign occupation. It would take until the late 1960s, and especially the early 1970s, for the Shah to feel and act as the master of his domain.

The most significant contribution of the Pahlavi shahs to the development of Iranian foreign policy was the revival of balance-of-power thinking in Iran, based on developing harmonious relations will all major regional and world powers. During Reza Shah's reign from 1925 to 1941, Iran attempted to expand its ties to Germany, France, and the United States to balance the superior power of Britain and the Soviet Union. During the second Pahlavi shah's reign, while Iran was officially in the pro-American camp, the Shah successfully built mutually beneficial partnerships with European powers and, in the last decade of his rule, in the 1970s, with the Soviet Union, China, and India. At the regional level, too, the Shah applied this strategy. He had built good relations with Saudi Arabia, which enabled him to act in the early 1970s as OPEC's leading price hawk. He had cordial relations with President Sadat of Egypt, King Hussein of Jordan, and working relations with Israel.

It was indeed a major achievement of the Pahlavi shahs, especially the second, that in their time a professional, educated foreign policy establishment emerged in Iran, knowledgeable about the world and capable of successfully engaging their counterparts in London, Paris, and Washington and, in the 1970s, Moscow, Peking, and New Delhi. In the Pahlavi era Iran established diplomatic relations and inaugurated embassies in over one hundred countries, spanning all continents. While some of the top positions in Iran's foreign policy establishment were reserved for those with close ties to the Pahlavi court, a merit-based system was instituted in which, irrespective of their political leanings, Iranian diplomats were chosen on the basis of their knowledge of foreign languages and international relations. The Pahlavi era produced hundreds of knowledgeable diplomats who succeeded in building harmonious working relations with all the major powers and with the most significant international organizations. To be sure, Mohammad Reza Shah had final say in all matters of Iranian foreign policy. Despite this fact, however, with eminent multilingual statesmen/diplomats such as Abbas-Ali Khalatbari, Ahmad Mirfendereski, and Fereydoun Hoveyda advising him, the Shah managed to build a foreign policy and military apparatus for Iran that rested on understanding the world's realities and using this to protect Iran's interests in the international arena. While the bulk of Iranian diplomats were secular, cosmopolitan, and "westernized" in their worldviews, a sizeable portion of the personnel, especially those posted in Iran's embassies in Arab countries, hailed from religious backgrounds. In building a professional foreign policy apparatus for Iran, the Pahlavi shahs did not, for the most part, apply an ideological litmus test as a requirement for entry into the foreign service. This was one of the main reasons for their success in instituting modern practices in the conduct of Iranian foreign policy. By the same token, as we will see below, one of the major shortcomings of Iranian foreign policy after the revolution has been the undoing of much of the hard-won tradition of professionalism in the country's foreign policy apparatus.

For the first decade after the revolution's victory, with Khomeini in firm command of the country, no reference could be found to the idea of Iran's "national interests." The forces of reactionary politics supplanted the focus on national interests with a zealous attachment to exporting Islamic revolution. A thorough overhaul of the country's foreign policy bureaucracy meant that almost all of Iran's learned and worldly diplomats were ejected from the foreign ministry and replaced by Islamist ideologues who saw their mission as bringing a revolutionary Islamist ideology to the region and to the world. This had a tremendously negative effect on the knowledge that Iranians possessed about the world.

PUSH AND PULL: IRAN'S EASTWARD DRIFT

Especially during the second term of his presidency, Rafsanjani had attempted to institute a national interest-based foreign policy in Iran. The high point of these efforts was his attempt to attract large-scale investment from the United States, especially directed at Iran's oil and gas sector. The Rafsanjani Administration's offer to the American oil company Conoco was the largest foreign investment contract Iran offered since the revolution, and topped $1 billion in value. The Clinton Administration was in no mood for rapprochement, however, and rebuffed this offer in March 1995. It rejected Iran's offer forcefully and imposed comprehensive economic sanctions on the country two months later. Prior to these sanctions, during Rafsanjani's presidency, American oil companies had become the largest purchasers of Iranian oil, as two-way trade topped $4 billion, making the United States Iran's largest trading partner.

Following the imposition of sanctions on Iran, the U.S. Congress took the policy of economic warfare to new heights by passing the Iran-Libya Sanctions Act in August 1996. The Act, which is still on the books, gave the President the authority to impose penalties on any foreign firm that invested more than $40 million—a minute sum—in Iran's oil and gas sector. The passage of ILSA, which drew immediate protests at the time from senior officials of all the major European and Asian countries, as well as Canada and Australia, was one of the main reasons that Iran deepened its ties to Europe, China and Russia, for they proved to be far more reliable partners for Iran. During Rafsanjani's presidency, Iran began large-scale importation of Russian armaments to refurbish its devastated military hardware. Similarly, it was in the 1990s, during the Rafsanjani and Khatami presidencies, that Iran developed multi-billion-dollar trade and investment relations with China. The high point of Iran's cooperation with China was the successful completion by the latter of Tehran's subway system in the late 1990s, a project whose foundations had been laid, similar to the country's nuclear program, in the 1970s by the Shah's government, albeit with American and European partners.

During Rafsanjani's presidency, Iran also attempted to buy a stake in the British Petroleum-led Azerbaijan International Operating Company, which was tasked after the dissolution of the Soviet Union with developing Azerbaijan's oil resources. Despite Iran's offer, however, U.S. opposition to Iran's involvement in AIOC induced Iran to deepen its partnerships with Russia and China. This tilt was buttressed by dogged U.S. opposition to the construction of new oil and gas pipelines through Iranian territory, despite the proven economic feasibility of the Iranian route. The record of Iran's rejected overtures to the United States throughout the 1990s shows that Iran's eastward tilt in the 1990s owed more to policies of the United States and its regional allies than to Iran's ideological preference for Asian partners. Viewed in this light, Iran was pushed toward Asia more than it was pulled in that direction. During this time, Iran's trade and security ties to China and Russia reached new heights. One of the most significant achievements of this time for Iran was the Chinese-led completion of the Tehran metro, which was completed in the late 1990s.

A few years later, the reality of Iran's partial eastward drift was put on display in July 2005, when Iran was invited by Shanghai Cooperation Organization (SCO) to attend a meeting of the heads of state of the seven-member organization in Astana, Kazakhstan's capital. The SCO, which is a security pact between China, Russia, and the four former Soviet Republics of Central Asia situated between them, was founded in 2001 as an attempt to counterbalance the expansion of U.S. economic and military influence in Central Asia. In a culmination of this policy, in 2005, the SCO invited India, Pakistan, and Iran to join the organization as observers. All three countries accepted and are now considering becoming full-fledged members of an organization whose raison d'etre has been to contain what its founders see as U.S. expansionism in their backyards. Photographed sitting across the negotiating table from China's president, Hu Jintao, was Mohammad Reza Aref, Iran's Stanford-educated first vice president who served under Khatami. This meeting, despite its importance, was ignored by the U.S. media and most foreign policy academics.

In June 15–16, 2006, less than one year after Iran's first participation in the organization, Mahmoud Ahmadinejad became the first Iranian president to join the SCO's deliberations. Commemorating the fifth anniversary of its founding, China had invited heads of state from Central Asian countries, as well as India, Pakistan, Iran and, of course, Russia to attend the SCO summit in Shanghai. At the meeting, Ahmadinejad delivered a speech in which he supported the organization's aims. He said, "the cooperation of the member states of the organization can have a positive effect on buttressing international peace and stability, and on blocking the illegal threats, interference, and the bullying inherent in the system of global domination." In a thinly veiled criticism of the United States and its allies, Ahmadinejad welcomed the alliance's focus on providing security for the Central Asian region. He discussed the cultural and historical depth of relations between Iran and the SCO's member states. Yet Ahmadinejad stopped short of committing Iran to full cooperation with the SCO.

He said, "[B]ased on its geopolitical and geo-economic position (he used the terms in English during his Persian speech) and by relying on its political and economic capacities, Iran declares its readiness for cooperating with member countries of the organization on the goals of bringing peace, lasting security, and the expansion of justice and welfare in the region." Ahmadinejad's reference to individual "member countries," as opposed to the organization itself, shows that his speechwriters were cognizant of the importance of maintaining Iran's independence from the SCO's founders, China and Russia, while cooperating with the organization in areas of mutual interest. Ahmadinejad's speech is a clear indication of the revival of balance-of-power thinking in Iran. Equally noteworthy is that his speech did not include a single reference to Islam, nor to the fact that Iran shares this faith with the four Central Asian countries that are SCO members.[5]

About four months after the SCO summit, which the American media once again ignored, Iran's foreign ministry think tank, the Institute for Political and International Studies, convened a conference in Tehran titled "The SCO: Prospects and Opportunities." Opening the conference, which was held on October 30–31, 2006, Iran's foreign minister Manuchehr Mottaki declared that "Central Asia is the missing link between East and West. This region, especially because it contains huge energy reserves, has become a locus of competition for the world's great powers . . . After the revolution of 1979, this is the first time that Iran is officially cooperating with a political-security-economic pact." Mottaki's remarks at the conference showed the same sensitivity to balance-of-power thinking. Another Iranian official participant at the event, Kazem Sajjadpour, who serves as Ambassador to Iran's Mission at the UN in Geneva, expanded on Mottaki's statements. He said, "The US was not sensitive to the SCO but became sensitive after Iran was accepted as an observer in June." Referring to the leading role played by China in the SCO, and the perception that the organization is focused on reducing U.S. influence in the region, Sajjadpour added that "Beijing and Washington both have concerns in this regard which each should pay attention to." Quoting figures from the Pentagon, Sajjadpour noted that China's military budget had been steadily increasing in the past years and had reached USD100 billion. Supporting the idea that Iran was in between east and west, and yet in neither's exclusive camp, Sajjadpour focused on the importance of cooperative Sino-American relations. He said the balance of U.S.-China trade was in Beijing's favor and that China enjoyed a 200-billion-dollar trade surplus with the United States. "China-US ties are not such as would lead Beijing to adopt anti-US moves and turn the SCO into an anti-American organization. So, it is an obvious mistake to think that the SCO is a cold war organization," Sajjadpour concluded.

The future of Iran's relationship with the SCO will be one of the yardsticks by which the direction of Iran's foreign policy will be judged in the next decade. In April 2002, Hu's predecessor, Jiang Zemin, had become the first Chinese leader to pay an official visit to Iran. In the current strategic environment, China's influence on Iranian foreign policy transcends trade and has—especially through the SCO—developed into a broader, eastern option for Iran.

Close to three months prior to the first SCO summit in which Iran participated, the Chinese Premier Wen Jiabao had paid a groundbreaking four-day state visit to India in April 2005. Showing the advancement of rapprochement between the two erstwhile rivals, Wen's trip can be seen as developing a Pan-Asian economic and security network that can address its need by relying on Asian countries, without reliance on extra-regional powers, especially the United States and some of its NATO allies.

Following on the heels of the SCO summit in July 2005, came another major sign of the changing geopolitics of Asia: in August 2005, for the first time in history, the People's Republic of China held joint military exercises with the Russian Federation. Incorporating their air, sea, and ground forces, the exercises were aimed at showing the resoluteness of Beijing and Moscow in expanding their strategic reach, especially in Central Asia. These two developments indicate that for the first time, a formidable "eastern" block has emerged, which incorporates half of the earth's population, and seems destined, especially due to China's rapid pace of economic growth, to become the world's largest trading block. While China and India were known up until two decades ago for making cheap toys and garments, they are now capable, especially together, of building aircraft carriers, refineries, nuclear reactors, and a range of advanced weapons. Adding Russia's capabilities to the mix makes the Asian bloc even more formidable.

It is now clear, in hindsight, that the attempted isolation and containment of Iran by the United States and European countries, evident in the reluctance of the vast majority of their heads of state to visit postrevolutionary Iran, stands in stark contrast to the assertive and adroit diplomacy of China, India, and to a lesser extent Russia, who have tried, successfully, to bring Iran into their economic and strategic orbit. In the case of China and India, in particular, their need for Iran's oil and gas resources is likely to further cement the depth of their ties to Iran.

The economic and geopolitical ramifications of Iran's eastward drift was covered in a feature length article in *Fortune Magazine* in February 2005.[6] According to the Fortune article, in a major two-part deal signed with China's Sinopec Group and other Chinese companies in October 2004, China has agreed to import large volumes of gas from Iran's South Pars field for the next thirty years, which is likely to make it Iran's largest gas customer in the near future. China's gas imports from Iran are estimated to generate over $70 billion over the next three decades. China has also negotiated a major stake in one of the largest oil fields in southwestern Iran, Yadavaran, enabling China to begin exploration work there. Together these contracts with China are slated to generate over $100 billion of revenue for Iran in the next few decades.

Iran's cooperation with Russia, another pillar of Iran's evolving foreign policy, has focused on nuclear energy and armaments. The bulk of Iran's military needs and its nuclear infrastructure have been met by Russia, a trend that began during Rafsanjani's presidency. More recently, Iran has begun naval cooperation with India, whose technicians have helped Iran maintain and modify its Russian-made submarines and other vessels in the Iranian navy.

Whereas in the last Shah's time there was little effective demand for partnerships that emanated from the East, beginning in the 1990s, corresponding with the phenomenal rise of China and, to a lesser extent India, the Eastern option is a reality that Iran can no longer ignore. In 2005 alone, Iran's trade with China reached $7 billion, making it by far Iran's largest trading partner. After awakening from the stupor of the Yelstin years under President Putin, Russia, too, has been more willing and capable to compete with the United States and its NATO allies over Iran and the region that surrounds it. In short, while reverting to the Shah's balance-of-power foreign policy, Iran finds itself in a radically different international environment where not only Russia, but also China, India, and Japan, as well as a number of Iran's neighbors, especially Turkey and Pakistan, increasingly craft their policies toward Iran on the basis of their national interests, which do not always correspond to the demands made by the United States to isolate Iran. In fact, increasingly they do not.

One of Iran's key priorities in the opening years of the new century has been to lay the groundwork for a network of gas pipelines to carry Iranian gas north to the Caucasus, west to Turkey, and most importantly, east to Pakistan and India. Driven by their burgeoning need for energy as their economies grow, Indian and Pakistani officials have repeatedly voiced their commitment to beginning work on the estimated $7 billion project. The United States, however, has opposed the building of the pipeline, harkening back to its opposition to the involvement of Iran in the Western-dominated Azerbaijan oil consortium in the early 1990s.

In late December and early January 2005/2006, in an unusually cold winter, supply shortages and price disputes forced a cut in the volume of Russian gas exports to the Ukraine and Georgia. Being in the vicinity of Iran, and intending to diversify its supply, in early January 2006 Georgia signed a preliminary agreement with Iran to import gas. Similarly, Turkey and Iran have been negotiating ways in which Iran meets a larger portion of the former's gas needs, which currently stand at about 20 percent.

In such a transformed world, characterized by an economically and militarily rising Asia, Iran finds itself, culturally and geopolitically, in between east and west. While Iran's relations with Asian powers have a much longer history than they do with most European countries and the United States, it is erroneous nonetheless to assume that Iran can successfully improve its domestic, regional, and international position without building steady and reliable partnerships with the United States and Europe, alongside its Asian partners. In the absence of American and European demand for its goods and services, Iran is bound to be at the mercy of China, Russia, and India, much the same way that it would be at the mercy of the West without an effective countervailing force from the East. This realization constitutes the core of balance-of-power thinking in Iran, based on realizing the fact that the country's comparative advantage is setting itself up, along with Turkey, as a bridge between east and west and, in Iran's particular case, between north and south, to and from the Persian Gulf and Caspian sea and their surrounding countries.

In this context, it is important to note that the United States remains the world's most advanced country technologically and militarily, and its largest economy. While Russia and China have made undeniable progress throughout the 1990s in meeting Iran's economic and military needs, it is unlikely that they possess the technology or the economic wherewithal to help Iran grow in the absence of substantial American and European involvement. Yet the United States and its European allies must increasingly acknowledge that Iran's eastward drift is serious and likely to continue until Western powers recognize that the hand of partnership extended by the last three Iranian presidents can no longer be dismissed or rebuffed. Such strategic and geopolitical vision must transcend the ideological shackles in Iran and among a few Western countries that have stymied progress on this front.

TURKO-PERSIAN REALM

Among all of Iran's neighbors, its relationship with Turkey, the modern heir to the Ottoman Empire, is the oldest and remains the most significant of all of Iran's regional ties. This is so for historical, cultural, geopolitical, and economic reasons. More than any other country in the world, modern Turkey's development has been intertwined with Iran's. To be sure, the attainment of détente between Turkey and Iran predates the founding of the modern Turkish Republic in 1923, and goes as far back as the time of the Iranian king Nader Shah's reign in the mid-eighteenth century. Yet it was in the twentieth century, especially after the Ottoman empire's dismemberment after World War I, that the two countries began to see their fates as intertwined. From the time of the founding of the modern Turkish Republic, peace has characterized relations between the two countries. During the 1980s, as Iran embraced a revolutionary foreign policy, its relations with Turkey soured noticeably. But beginning in the 1990s, with democracy advancing in Turkey, and with Iran's reversion to a national interest-based foreign policy, relations have steadily grown. The deep rapprochement between the two countries came about in 2003 with the American- and British-led invasion of Iraq.

One of the most significant reasons behind the truce between Iran and the Ottoman Empire, from the mid-eighteenth century onward, was the expanded power of the British and Russian Empires in the Turkish-Iranian region. Having been involved in numerous wars with Russia to its northeast, and with European powers on its western flank, the Ottomans had come to realize that Persia was not the main threat to their regional ambitions. This lingering fear would prove well-founded in the early twentieth century during World War I, as Great Britain captured all Ottoman territories in current-day Iraq, which led to the dissolution of the Ottoman empire, ending its five centuries of regional dominance, whose imperial and artistic achievements have been enshrined in the majestic palaces and mosques of Istanbul, and elsewhere in Turkey.

For two and a half centuries, the Ottoman and Safavid empires had been roughly equal rivals, wielding a similar level of military power, while they both held large territories. Beginning in the mid-eighteenth century, however, and extending until the early twentieth, this parity no longer existed. While Iran's territory steadily shrunk and the country's cohesion showed steady erosion, the Ottomans remained strong and well organized throughout the eighteenth and nineteenth centuries as they reigned undisputed over what is today's Iraq, much of today's Saudi Arabia, as well as over what is current-day Turkey and farther west.

As we saw in the first section, during the four years of World War I, Iran was a country only in name, as it lacked a standing army that could enforce its territorial integrity. All the fledgling Iranian government could do during World War I was to declare its neutrality. This did not prevent warring parties, however, from using Iranian territory, especially in western Iran, to attack each other's positions. During that war the Ottomans, in stark contrast, fielded an army of 300,000 men. The Ottomans were members of an alliance that included the major powers of Germany and the Austro-Hungarian empire. One of their leaders, an Ottoman "Pasha" (Turkish for general) who successfully held back the British advance at Gallipoli during the war, was Mustapha Kemal, who became the first president of the newly founded Republic of Turkey in 1923.

Mustapha Kemal Ataturk was a hero to Iran's Reza Shah. In the summer of 1934, at the peak of his powers, Reza Shah made the only official foreign trip of his sixteen-year reign. He visited Ankara and other Turkish cities for a full month, searching for innovative ways of advancing his own modernization drive in Iran. When the train carrying Reza Shah and the two dozen Iranian officials and journalists who were accompanying him arrived at the Ankara train station, they were greeted by thousands of Turkish well-wishers who had been assembled to welcome the Shah. Turkish and Iranian flags adorned many sections of the Turkish capital, especially all official sites, and the Turkish press called Reza Shah Turkey's "great guest." In the words of Abbas Masudi, the founding editor of the Iranian daily, *Ettelaat*, who was on the Iranian delegation, "the entire population of the city has crowded onto the streets of the capital to welcome the Shah."[7]

Standing on the platform of the Ankara train station to officially welcome the Shah were Ataturk and numerous senior Turkish officials. An honor guard fired a 21-gun salute and played the Iranian national anthem. On the first evening of his arrival in Anakara, Reza Shah and his delegation took part in a gala dinner reception hosted by Ataturk at his presidential quarters, the Chankaya. This was the first chance that the two men had to become acquainted with one another in person. Since Reza Shah had a good command of Azeri-Turkish, there was no need for translators. It was during the first days of his stay in Ankara that Atraturk invited Reza Shah to extend his trip, a request the Shah accepted. His four-week stay, which included tours across the country, holds the record as the longest official visit of an Iranian leader to another country in the twentieth century.

At the gala reception held in the Chankaya, Ataturk raised a toast to his guest:

With the greatest pleasure we welcome the leader of our brother nation, Alahazrat Humayun [Reza Shah's title] upon his arrival in Turkey. The entire Turkish nation is honored by His Majesty's presence. Whenever in history these two nations have been at odds they have experienced the most difficult periods of their existence. However, whenever they have worked together they have made progress. The Turkish republic considers good relations with Iran to be central to its politics ... and the friendship which day by day between these two brother nations advances ... our nations will go down the the road of peace and be part of the global peace which is our hope.[8]

Reza Shah's trip included a tour of Istanbul. He visited the Istanbul Museum, the Hagia Sophia mosque and the Turkish military academy, where he was further educated about the Turkish war of independence. At the Iranian consulate in Istanbul, before a sizeable gathering of Iranian residents of Istanbul, Reza Shah said:

The thing which has been so much a source of happiness during this trip has been the unity which has been shown between the Turkish and Iranian nations. Henceforth you must think of Turkey as your second nation and Turks as your brothers ... I am hopeful that henceforth these two nations will give each other their hand in harmony and have confidence in each other as they live and coexist in happiness and progress.[9]

One of the pillars of the strong bond between Reza Shah and Ataturk was the fact that they had both been career military men. Before assuming the mantle of leadership, both had felt the humiliation of extra-regional powers' encroachment on their domains. At the same time, both men knew that the path of development required internalizing the achievements of the West, and overcoming the legacy of religious rule which, in their views, had retarded their nations' progress. Similar to Ataturk, in the 1920s, Reza Shah had tried, albeit unsuccessfully, to become the first president of his country. Coming on the heels of centuries of traditional and religiously sanctioned rule by sultans and shahs in their respective countries, Ataturk and Reza Shah were harbingers of modern nationhood in Turkey and Iran, even if as a professional military man, Reza Shah knew he was outclassed by Ataturk. Since Ataturk and Reza Shah were the most important figures of twentieth-century Turkey and Iran respectively, their deep bonds of admiration, especially of Reza Shah toward Ataturk, laid the foundations of the deep contemporary bonds between the two countries.

In the present time, Iran's relationship with Turkey should be seen, similarly, as the most important focus of the country's regional foreign policy, for two main reasons. First is the cultural affinity between the two countries. About a third of Iran's population, close to 25 million Iranians, speak Turkish as a mother tongue, while being fluent in Persian, Iran's official language. The Turkish-speaking population of Iran, while concentrated in Azerbaijan, is present in large numbers across many of the country's northeastern and western provinces. They constitute the heart of the Turko-Persian realm as they are Turkish and Persian in their roots, and Iranian in their nationality. Simply put, there is no country with which Iranians feel as much cultural affinity.

For more than eight hundred years in the last millennium, it was Turkic dynasties who ruled Iran. Without their dedication to protecting Iran's territorial and cultural integrity, it is doubtful that the country would have survived in its present form. This was especially so in the case of the Safavid dynasty. And, closer to our own time, many of the leading political and cultural leaders of twentieth-century Iran have hailed from Azeri backgrounds: Sattar Khan, Bagher Khan, Hassan Taghizadeh, Ahmad Kasravi, Fereidun Jam, among many others, are widely known as leading Iranian nationalists in the twentieth century. Factoring out Turkish-speaking people's contributions to Iranian history would indeed be tantamount to the hollowing out of Iran. In that sense, the relationship between Turkish and Iranian peoples is one of deep and historically grounded interdependence. World history's leading mystical poet, Rumi, wrote in Persian about eight centuries ago; he is buried in Konya in eastern Turkey.

The second reason for the importance of Iran's relationship with Turkey is that Turkey is Iran's bridge to the west *and* to the east. Geographically speaking, any attempt by Iran to export its goods, especially its gas, to Europe will have to cross Turkish territory as the most economically feasible route. At the same time, across Iran's northeast and into the Turkic republics of Central Asia, and extending as far as Western China, Turkish is spoken by 150 million people in numerous dialects. Similarly, to the south of the Turkish belt, a Persian language belt extends from Iran eastward to Afghanistan and continues on to Tajikistan. Not only in Iran itself, but also across Central Asia, Turkish and Persian, as languages and civilizations, have been superimposed for millennia. For the first time, after two world wars and a cold war that prevented this from happening, the Turkish and Iranian civilizations' affinity, if properly channeled, has the chance to enrich both countries significantly.

Turkey also has a great stake in good neighborly relations with Iran, and in deepening economic, security, and political cooperation between the two countries. In this area, three issues are key: Turkey's reliance on natural gas and other fuels from Iran, Turkey's interest in expanding its reach in the Caspian region through Iran, and Turkey's concern over containing separatist tendencies among its Kurdish population, who number close to 15 million in Turkey, over 20 percent of Turkey's population. Viewed more generally, under the leadership of Prime Minister Recep Tayyip Erdogan, who has been prime minister since March 2003, Turkey has attempted, in the early years of the twenty-first century, to become more actively, and more independently, involved in its own region, of which Iran is an integral part. Iran and Turkey are Central Eurasia's most populous and most deeply rooted republics. Their alliance, more than any other, promises to bring stability and development to the region that surrounds them.

One of the key objectives of current Turkish foreign policy is to become an energy hub to transport oil and natural gas from the Persian Gulf and Caspian Sea regions to Europe. This policy is evident in Prime Minsiter Erdogan's numerous visits to Ashgabat, Turkmenistan during 2006–2007.

One sign of Turkey's evolving foreign policy was the Saudi King Abdullah's visit to Ankara and Istanbul in November 2006, during which Turkey and Saudi Arabia signed numerous memoranda of understanding to expand investment and trade between the two countries. While the European Union debates whether to admit Turkey, seeing it as a large, but relatively poor and predominantly Muslim nation, Erdogan has been active in courting key countries in Turkey's own region. In 2006 alone, he visited Qatar, Bahrain, Pakistan, and other countries. To show Turkey's independent foreign policy, in February 2006 Erdogan hosted Khaled Mashaal, the leader of Hamas, which is a militant Palestinian group. In March 2006, Erdogan became the first Turkish leader to address a gathering of the Arab League. He has also condemned Israel's war on Hezbollah in Lebanon in the summer of 2006.[10]

Turkey's "eastern option," similar to Iran's, is based on its slow progress in becoming a member of the EU. Simultaneously, the American-British-led invasion of Iraq in March 2003 was very unpopular in Turkey, one of the reasons Turkish military and political leaders, despite their pro-Western leanings, did not acquiesce to American demands to use Turkish territory to open a northern flank in its invasion of Iraq.

Turkey is well on the path to crafting an independent foreign policy in which its own interests will take priority over those of its traditional allies, including the United States. Viewed in this light, Turkish-Iranian relations are a natural embodiment of this vision of Turkey of its place in the region that surrounds it and beyond. Similar to Iran, Turkey sees itself as a bridge between East and West. In the absence of solid ties to Iran, that vision of Turkey would be significantly set back. How can both countries see themselves as bridges between East and West, while not acknowledging the other as their main regional ally?

If Iran and Turkey continue their current path toward regional cooperation, they can exercise far greater influence in the "Turko-Persian realm": a vast area that extends from Western Turkey to Western China and incorporates over 250 million people, whose language and religion bind them in significant ways. At a time when the post-Cold War era has unleashed a quest for identity among newly independent peoples, it is important to remember that identity crises often breed instability and war. Greater contact and immersion in the Turko-Persian realm can enable newly independent Central Asian republics and Afghanistan to successfully connect to their roots, and to work toward a political and security architecture in which regional problems can meet regional solutions. Why should NATO or the SCO be burdened with bringing security to Central Asia and Afghanistan when this task can be accomplished, far more naturally, and with far less expense, within the Turko-Persian realm, anchored in a Turkish-Iranian alliance. For the Turko-Persian realm to work in practice, however, it will have to maintain its autonomy from the major powers. Neither Turkey's membership in NATO, nor Iran's observer status in the SCO should prevent them from pursuing a regional and international policy that looks to each other, first and foremost, for help and mutual benefit.

Three significant developments in May 2006 indicated that a Turko-Persian realm is indeed in the making. First was a meeting, in Baku on May 4, 2006, of the member states of the Economic Development Organization (ECO), which aims to promote interdependence and free trade among Turkey, Iran, Pakistan, the five Central Asian republics, Afghanistan, and Azerbaijan. ECO was founded by Turkey, Iran, and Pakistan in 1985 to facilitate interaction among member states, but due to the challenges posed by Iran's revolutionary stance in the 1980s, and the opposition of much of the world to Iran's destabilizing influence at that time, relations between Iran and the two other founders of ECO remained lukewarm for a decade after its establishment. The Baku meeting of ECO, however, showed that Turkey and Iran were indeed committed to expanding their cooperation within the organization's framework.

At the Baku meeting, while Turkey, Iran, Azerbaijan, and Afghanistan were represented by Prime Minister Erdogan, President Ahmadinejad, President Aliev, and President Karzai respectively, Pakistan and the Central Asian republics sent lower-ranking officials. These officials renewed their commitment to energize the organization and proposed new measures for coordinated action in meeting regional challenges. This meeting showed, once more, that Turkey and Iran are the two key pillars of the organization, whose cooperation and partnership is indispensable for regional stability and progress.

The second indication for the emergence of a Turko-Persian realm was a simultaneous and coordinated gathering of many thousands of Iranian and Turkish troops, in the second week of May 2006, along their respective borders with Iraq. This uncommon joint show of force by Turkey and Iran indicated that the two countries have a common stake in the stability and territorial integrity of Iraq, and that they view ethnically-based secessionist movements within their borders, especially in their Kurdish regions, with great alarm, as they are worried that this will threaten their territorial integrity. The coordinated Turkish-Iranian military exercises are significant since Turkish military leaders, while generally sympathetic to the needs of Turkey's NATO partners, had not agreed to the U.S. demand to use Turkish territory for its invasion of Iraq in March 2003.

While Turkey remains one of the main regional allies of the United States, it has sent a clear signal to the United States that it cannot see its relationship with Iran solely on the basis of the continuing deadlock in U.S.-Iran relations. In a related vein, former Turkish prime minister Bulent Ejevit, and the country's most prominent elder statesman, was quoted as having said to the Turkish daily *Yeni Shafaq* that the United States has opposed amicable ties between Turkey and Iran. "The United States is creating crises in this very sensitive strategic region of the world, that is a potential threat for Turkey and the entire region," Ejevit was quoted as saying. "During my years at service—four years ago—too, the Americans were warning Ankara not to establish amicable ties with Tehran. Iran has been Turkey's neighbor for over five hundred years and the cultural and artistic relations between the two nations need to be further expanded."[11]

The third recent indication that the idea of a Turko-Persian realm has received a boost comes from a summit of the D-8 organization in Bali, Indonesia on May 12, 2006. The D-8, which was founded by the then Turkish prime minister Nejmeddin Erbakan in 1997, includes six Asian countries—Turkey, Iran, Pakistan, Bangladesh, Indonesia, and Malaysia—and two African ones, Egypt and Nigeria. Similar to the previous week's ECO meeting in Baku, Erdogan and Ahmadinejad represented their countries at the summit. Ahmadinejad's advocacy of Iran's right to peaceful use of nuclear energy made him the focus of attention at the D-8 summit, which came on the heels of his three-day official visit to Jakarta, where he received an exceptionally warm welcome by the Indonesian public. Meanwhile, Indonesia has added its name to the list of countries that have proposed to mediate between the United States and Iran, hoping for a peaceful resolution of the deadlock.

In the wake of over seven decades of extensive bureaucratic development in Iran—from Reza Shah's time to the present—a modern foreign policy apparatus has matured in the country that, similar to all modern bureaucracies, is driven by its own rational calculus, as opposed to revolutionary and otherworldly concerns. This, as Max Weber showed, is the inescapable nature of modern bureaucracies.

The external reason for the emergence of an assertive, national interest-based foreign policy in Iran is the current international environment. At the time of the Iranian revolution, the global distribution of power was far less fluid, and far more predictable and certain than it is today. The emergence of China as a world power in the past quarter century; the expanding power of Russia and India; the advent of the eurozone encompassing over 400 million people, which, for the first time in postwar history, has emerged as a viable competitor to the U.S. dollar; the rise of antiglobalization movements on all continents; Islamic political movements from Egypt to Indonesia; dwindling U.S. popularity across the world—these and many other new realities have created an international environment and a balance of power in the international arena that are, on the whole, favorable to regional powers such as Iran and Turkey, who have a chance to create a balance of power of their own to be able to deliver security and development for their citizens.

CHAPTER THREE

New Directions in Iranian Foreign Policy

INTRODUCTION

As we have seen so far in this book, the greatest challenge facing Iranian foreign policy in the post-Khomeini era has been to rectify the damage that had been inflicted on the country's relationship with the international community in the 1980s. At that time, it had seemed that Iran had been transformed, almost overnight, from what President Carter had called an "island of stability" to a source of religious radicalism and violent revolution in its own region and beyond. We saw, also, that the Iranian revolution itself, the most consequential mass movement in Iranian history, had not been based on xenophobic sentiments as it had enjoyed the support of diverse strata, including the modern urban and educated middle class, and had contained secular, nationalist, and religious forces alike. Yet the takeover of the U.S. embassy in Tehran in early November 1979 completely derailed the progressive potential of the revolution, and brought to the fore xenophobic forces, each aiming to show the others that their camp was the most illiberal, anti-American, and anti-imperialist.

During the Iran-Iraq war in the 1980s, while Iraq enjoyed the indispensable financial backing of Saudi Arabia and its smaller allies in the newly formed Gulf Cooperation Council, and received massive shipments of armaments from the Soviet Union, China, France, Germany, the UK, as well as strategic help from the United States, Iran mostly fought the war alone. It seems clear in retrospect that Iran in the 1980s had chosen to take on the whole world. Iraq had also received a chemical weapons manufacturing capacity from numerous countries, which it used on tens of thousands of Iranian soldiers and civilians beginning in the mid-1980s. The United Nations Security Council, compelled by the above powers to oppose Iran, refused to call Iraq the aggressor in the war, even though it was clear that Iraq's invasion of Iran on September 22, 1980 had started the war. Nor did the UNSC demand that Iraq withdraw from Iranian territory, where Iraqi forces remained as occupiers until 1982.

Nineteen years after the end of the Iran-Iraq war, the bitter memories of that war are still present in the thoughts of Iranian officials. The Iranian foreign minister Manuchehr Mottaki's speech before the UN Security Council on March 23, 2007, offers solid corroboration for this claim. Addressing the UN body in New York after it imposed a new round of sanctions on Iran's nuclear and military programs, Mottaki claimed:

> This is not the first time the Security Council is asking Iran to abandon its rights. When Saddam Hussein invaded Iran 27 years ago, this Council waited seven days so that Iraq could occupy 30,000 sq kilometers of Iranian territory. Then it unanimously adopted Security Council Resolution 479. That unanimously adopted resolution asked the two sides to stop the hostilities, without asking the aggressor to withdraw. That is, the Council—then too—effectively asked Iran to suspend the implementation of parts of its rights; at that time it was its right to 30,000 sq kilometers of its territory. As expected, the aggressor dutifully complied. But imagine what would have happened if Iran had complied. We would still be begging the Council's then sweetheart, President Saddam Hussein, to return our territory. We did not accept to suspend our right to our territory. We resisted eight years of carnage and use of chemical weapons coupled with pressure from this Council, and sanctions from its permanent members.
>
> In the course of the war, the United States joined the United Kingdom, Germany, France, and the Soviet Union along with other Western countries in providing Saddam with military hardware and intelligence and even the material for chemical and biological weapons. The Security Council was prevented for several years and in spite of mounting evidence and UN reports, to deal with the use of chemical weapons by Iraq against Iranian civilians and military personnel. I am confident that today, most of the permanent members of this Council, do not even want to remember that travesty of justice, the Charter and international law, let alone blame Iran for non-compliance with SCR 479.[1]

While it is natural for Iran to feel aggrieved by the actions of the major powers during the Iran-Iraq war, it is also important to remember that Iran was seen at the time, by most of the international community, as a reckless and irrational actor in international affairs, whose otherworldly and "martyrdom-seeking" agenda was threatening to the region surrounding Iran, and beyond. Hostage taking, suicide bombings, and acts of terror backed by Iran were not limited to the war fronts with Iraq. The crucial support Iran provided to the militant wings of the Hezbollah movement in Lebanon sent the signal that Iran was not interested in observing any rules. This was part of the reason that the richest of the Arab monarchies in the Persian Gulf, threatened by Khomeini's call for Islamic revolution in their countries, provided Saddam Hussein with over $50 billion in direct financial support, much of which was used to acquire modern weapons for Iraqi forces to be used against Iranians. The radicalism of Iran's foreign policy was matched by the murderous treatment of the clerical system's domestic opponents within Iran and abroad. In August 1988 alone, close to five thousand people in Iranian prisons were summarily executed for posing a political threat to the Islamic Republic. Throughout the 1980s, the number of people executed for political offences reached tens of thousands. How could the international system feel sympathy for a country whose leaders saw the deaths of their people, and the destruction of their country's infrastructure, as a path to heaven?

During the eight years of war with Iraq, Iranian forces repeatedly mounted "final offensives" and expended much blood as they wished to first liberate the holy city of Karbala from Saddam's rule, and then march on Jerusalem and liberate it from "Zionists." With their thinking clouded by religious zeal, little did Iranian leaders recognize at the time that the world's most powerful countries who were threatened by Iran's export of radicalism would not allow Iran to make significant headway, even if it meant supporting Saddam Hussein, who was already infamous for his human rights violations within and beyond his borders. Indeed, such are the dangers of uneducated religious zeal.

Following the election of Mahmoud Ahmadinejad, a religious conservative, as Iran's president in August 2005, and judging by his harsh rhetoric, many observers wonder whether Iran has reverted to the irrational behavior of the 1980s. Many of Ahmadinejad's speeches to domestic audiences are replete with otherworldly references to "the coming judgment day," "the necessity of following the prophet's path," and his repeated reference to the "divine system of the Islamic Republic," have signaled that Iranian leaders continue justifying their deeds by reference to the words and the will of God. Indeed, Iran remains the only country in the world whose leaders resort to otherworldly references while responding to their domestic and international opponents. Similarly, Iran is the only country whose people are goaded by their political leaders to chant "Death to America," "Death to Israel," and "Death to Britain," depending on the political exigencies of the day. These are distinctions that one hopes Iran will one day leave behind. How would Iranians feel, it is worth asking, if other countries' leaders made it part of their routine political discourse to chant such slogans at Iran?

Our aim in this chapter is to show that in the post-Khomeni era, especially during the two-term presidencies of Rafsanjani and Khatami, under the leadership of Khamenei, Iran largely succeeded in overcoming the destructive legacy of the 1980s. Thus, while Ahmadinejad and like-minded individuals in Iran's security and military establishment use harsh rhetoric to buttress their revolutionary credentials, most Iranians and the majority of the country's political leaders have evolved and seek a peaceful symbiosis with the international community.

To be sure, a close scrutiny of the current Iranian president shows that there are two Ahmadinejads: one harkening back to the revolutionary zeal of the 1980s, and the other signifying the steady progress of reform in Iran in the past seventeen years. For every radical statement Ahmadinejad has made, he has uttered an equal number on the need for "brotherly love," the peaceful nature of the Iranian people, and his utmost respect for other faiths, especially Christianity and Judaism. In international forums, especially, one can easily see that the more moderate and rational Ahmadinejad holds sway. Having built up his revolutionary credentials, Ahmadinejad and his kindred spirits are in a position to adopt a more pragmatic and moderate approach vis-à-vis the international community, since they cannot be charged by their domestic opponents as being "soft on imperialism."

It seems that Iranian leaders take refuge in otherworldly rhetoric when they feel backed into a corner by the major powers, especially the United States. At the same time, Iran's body politic has reached enough maturity to realize the major threat that religious extremism poses to international stability and Iran's evolving place in the international order. It is as though Ahmadinejad and his ilk are saying, "If they don't include us in international arrangements, we will respond like we did in the 1980s." In this sense, it seems as though some Iranian leaders' rhetoric is designed as a scare tactic to deal with their international opponents, and is intended to goad Iran's adversaries to accept the country's place in the international community. Very much unlike the 1980s, however, the radical statements of Iranian leaders do not emanate from a rigid ideology and actual belief; rather, harsh rhetoric is being used as a tactical ploy by the country's political leadership to gain short-term advantage. The challenge of progress for Iranians is to stop pretending that Iran can, under any circumstances, turn the clock back and return to the fanatical zeal of the 1980s.

AHMADINEJAD'S LETTERS TO AMERICA: DECIPHERING THE FOREIGN POLICY THINKING OF IRANIAN LEADERS

President Mahmoud Ahmadinejad's two open letters to America, first to President George W. Bush (written in early May 2006) and the other to the American people (written in late November 2006, after the mid-term U.S. congressional elections) represent the two diametrically opposed sides of his thinking. In his long letter to President Bush, for example, Ahmadinejad presents a series of rhetorical questions that amount to a fundamental critique of American and Israeli foreign policy. While his letter is replete with references to divine prophets, Ahmadinejad makes no attempt at all to address the current sources of tension between the two countries: Iran's nuclear program, Iran's need for energy, including nuclear energy, U.S.-imposed sanctions and the general U.S. policy of containing Iran, and the tension between the two countries over Iraq, Lebanon, and across the Middle East. The content and tone of the letter was such that it made it very difficult to respond to the issues he raised. Deeply steeped in rhetoric, his questions are actually statements that amount to lecturing President Bush on international relations and U.S. foreign policy. These may be some of the reasons why President Bush chose not respond to Ahmadinejad's letter.

It seems that Ahmadinejad's advisers failed to tell him that those Americans who would actually sit down to read his letters are likely to be educated, liberally minded people with secular leanings. Such people would not look kindly upon the Iranian president's incessant references in his letters to "God," "Divine Prophets: Moses, Jesus, and Mohammad," and numerous otherworldly references. In fact, such references to the afterlife are likely to negatively affect the American readers of Ahmadinejad's letters who see him through these letters as an irrational and dogmatic individual, if not a religious fanatic.

Immediately after Ahmadinejad's letter to Bush, China's state-run news agency, Xinhua, quoted Ahmadinejad as saying that he awaited a response from the U.S. president. "We will wait to see what would be the reaction of the other side and then we will make the decision."[2] A few days after Ahmadinejad's claim that he sought a response from the United States, Ahmad Moussavi, Iran's vice president for legal and parliamentary affairs, was quoted as saying that "if Bush gives a fair and reasoned reply to Ahmadinejad's letter, we will welcome it and regard it as a step in diplomacy and forging of understanding."[3]

While it is understandable why President Bush chose not to respond to the letter, it seems that a simple note of acknowledgment by President Bush would have sent a signal that the United States is open to dialogue, as opposed to suggesting that the United States doesn't wish to dignify the letter with a response, or that it prefers snubbing the outreach of the president of a developing country. In such a hypothetical response, President Bush may have acknowledged having read the Iranian president's long letter, and then he could have responded to Ahmadinejad's charges by claiming that the Iranian president's letter conveniently ignores those aspects of Iran's domestic and international behavior that the United States and numerous other countries find troubling: Iran's nuclear program that might have military applications, its support for militant, anti-Israel groups, its support of violent militias in Iraq, etc.

In his second letter to America, addressed to the American public, Ahmadinejad, following in the footsteps of his predecessor Mohammad Khatami, repeatedly addresses the "Noble American people." In the opening to this letter, Ahmadinejad claims,

> While divine providence has placed Iran and the United States geographically far apart, we should be cognizant that human values and our common human spirit, which proclaim the dignity and exalted worth of all human beings, have brought our two great nations of Iran and the United States closer together. Both our nations are God-fearing, truth-loving and justice-seeking, and both seek dignity, respect and perfection. Both greatly value and readily embrace the promotion of human ideals such as compassion, empathy, respect for the rights of human beings, securing justice and equity, and defending the innocent and the weak against oppressors and bullies. We are all inclined towards the good, and towards extending a helping hand to one another, particularly to those in need. We all deplore injustice, the trampling of peoples' rights and the intimidation and humiliation of human beings. We all detest darkness, deceit, lies and distortion, and seek and admire salvation, enlightenment, sincerity and honesty. The pure human essence of the two great nations of Iran and the United States testify to the veracity of these statements.

> Noble Americans,
>   Our nation has always extended its hand of friendship to all other nations of the world. Hundreds of thousands of my Iranian compatriots are living amongst you in friendship and peace, and are contributing positively to your society. Our people

have been in contact with you over the past many years and have maintained these contacts despite the unnecessary restrictions of US authorities.

Ahmadinejad's letter to the American people, as the above quotes make clear, represent the more conciliatory side of the Iranian president's thinking. What is noteworthy in Ahmadinejad's letters is that he never mentions the word "Islam"; nor does he refer to "Islamic unity," "Islamic nation," and other references that were hallmarks of the Iranian leadership's pronouncements throughout the 1980s. It is safe to assume that unlike the Khomeini years, when millions of Iranians and their leaders were actually enraptured by the calls for Islamic revolution, in their own country and abroad, the current instances of otherworldly rhetoric are hollow attempts at convincing the international community to accept Iran as a significant actor on the world stage.

The key issue for the international community to realize is that the only way to bring Iran into the fold is by engaging its people, including its political leadership. Attempts at pushing Iran into a corner, sanctions, and worst of all military action against Iran, will undoubtedly bring out the revolutionary and destructive side of the Iranian leadership, and they will ignite, as they did in the 1980s, the xenophobic undercurrent of the Iranian psyche. It is here that the restoration of diplomatic relations between the United States and Iran assumes special significance. The international community, especially the United States as the world's leading power, would be better off if they ceased referring to Iran as "terrorist sponsor," and if they did not pepper every official statement about Iran with a litany of charges against it, as though they were addressing a criminal.

At the same time, it is undeniable that some of the policies of the United States and its allies in the region that surrounds Iran are currently the worst possible remedies for containing the remaining currents of extremism in Iran. Resorting to military force by the United States and its allies will doom Iran and the region that surrounds it to another generation of war and destruction. Today's Iran, after two decades of sanctions and various other forms of isolation, is similar to a powder keg that, though contained for the moment, could easily burst and damage all that it finds in its path—an outcome that would be especially disastrous for Iran itself.

IRAN AND THE GCC

To grasp the areas in which Iran has succeeded in overcoming the excesses of the 1980s, it is necessary to discuss Iran's relations with countries that were locked in bitter disputes with Iran in the first decade after the 1979 revolution's victory. Nowhere is this truer than in Iran's ties to the pro-American monarchies of the Persian Gulf and the Arabian peninsula. During the Iran-Iraq war, Khomeini had said that Iran would "never" seek peace with Saudi Arabia—Saddam Hussein's main financial backer during the 1980s. Yet beginning in the mid-1990s, Iran successfully overcame the legacy of the 1980s, and it succeeded in building a mutually beneficial relationship with the Saudi Kingdom, and its smaller allies in the Gulf Cooperation Council, which include Kuwait, the United Arab Emirates, Qatar, Bahrain, and Oman. Since the 1990s, Iran's relations with all members of the GCC have improved significantly. It is fair to claim that GCC members, especially Saudi Arabia, no longer see Iran as a source of tension and ideological warfare in the region the way they once did.

Under the tutelage of the United States and the UK, the GCC was created in 1981 as a specific response to the shock waves unleashed by the Iranian revolution, as protection against Iranian adventurism. While Khomeini and his followers had repeatedly called for kindred spirits, especially the Shia, in GCC countries to revolt against their pro-American leaders, since Khoemeni's passing Iran has succeeded in undoing the damage that had been inflicted on its relations with its sea neighbors in the Persian Gulf and the Sea of Oman.

The door to détente with Saudi Arabia, the important actor in the GCC, was opened by the then president Rafsanjani's visit to Saudi Arabia in 1996 in the last year of his presidency. That trip was followed a year later by the then crown prince Abdullah's highly significant trip to Tehran on December 10–11, 1997, to take part in the meeting of the Organization of the Islamic Conference. That trip, the first by a senior Saudi leader to Iran since the revolution, solidified Saudi-Iranian ties. In his speech at the OIC conference in Tehran, Abdullah said:

It gives me pleasure on this auspicious occasion to convey to you the greetings of your brother, the Custodian of the Two Holy Mosques, King Fahd Ibn Abdulaziz, and his heartfelt congratulations to you and to Muslims at large at this blessed meeting.

Likewise, I am pleased to extend to you personally my best wishes and those of the Muslim people of Saudi Arabia. My profound thanks and appreciation to His Excellency, brother President Sayed Muhammad Khatami, for the warm welcome and generous hospitality with which we have been received since our arrival in this hospitable country. I would like to praise highly the great efforts made by His Excellency and his assistants in preparing for this Conference. May Allah Almighty secure for this meeting the success we all hope for and make it rise to the expectations pinned by the Muslim Nation on the leaders who are meeting here today.

With the immortal achievements credited to the Muslim people of Iran, and their invaluable contributions throughout our glorious Islamic history, it is no wonder that Teheran, the capital of the Islamic Republic of Iran, is hosting this important Islamic gathering; it is quite natural for the leadership of this Muslim country to be quite aware of its duties and responsibilities towards the Islamic Nation at this critical juncture in our common history; and, motivated by this feeling, to do all that is in its power to serve Islam and the Muslims, to consecrate the spirit of solidarity and interdependence among them, and to help them avoid all that may split their ranks or weaken their common cause.[4]

Less than two years later, in his trip to Riyadh in May 1999, the then president Mohammad Khatami emphasized the areas of mutual interest between the countries and sought ways of furthering cooperation between them. While Iran and Saudi Arabia had worked at cross-purposes in the 1980s in the economic and political realms, the new détente that was achieved between them enabled them to focus on cooperation, instead of competition, in their own region and beyond.

To be sure, the religious competition between Iran and Saudi Arabia lingered throughout the 1990s. Nowhere was this more evident than in the financial backing provided by Saudi Arabia to the Taliban movement in Afghanistan in the latter half of that decade. The Taliban's religious extremism was especially directed against Iranians' Shia Muslim faith, which the Taliban's leaders considered heretical. The confrontation between Iran and the Taliban reached a peak in the summer of 1998 when the Taliban attacked the Iranian consulate in the predominantly Shia town of Mazar-e-Sahrif and murdered eleven diplomats stationed there, along with thousands of residents. Such acts by the Taliban did not convince Saudi Arabia and some of its GCC allies, especially the UAE, to cease their support for the Taliban. It was only after the American-led invasion of Afghanistan, and the overthrow of the Taliban that this serious point of contention between Saudi Arabia and Iran was removed.

Another high point in the rapprochement between Iran and Saudi Arabia came in March 2007, when President Ahmadinejad accepted Saudi King Abdullah's invitation to visit Riyadh. In a rare gesture reserved for Saudi Arabia's closest allies, King Abdullah greeted the Iranian president at the Riyadh airport and was pictured holding Ahmadinejad's hand as they walked from the tarmac. During Ahmadinejad's trip, the Saudi press referred to the two countries as "brotherly nations," and hailed Ahmadinejad's visit as another sign of deepening ties between the two countries. Prior to this visit, Saudi National Security Advisor, Prince Bandar bin-Sultan, among the most pro-American figures in the country's leadership, had made a trip to Tehran to voice his government's interest in building harmonious relations with Iran.

The most significant reason for the rapprochement between Iran and Saudi Arabia since the 1990s has been the fact that Iran has steadily distanced itself from the militant and revolutionary zeal that had characterized it in the 1980s. As a matter of policy, Iranian leaders no longer question the Islamic legitimacy of the Saudi Kingdom and have dropped their claims to being the only legitimate interpreters and practitioners of Islam.

At the same time, Saudi Arabia has, in the past decade, especially since King Abdullah's accession to the throne in August 2005, attempted to demonstrate its independence from the United States. This was evident in the first foreign trip that Abdullah made as king: he visited China in January 2006 and promoted a deepening of Chinese-Saudi relations. Abdullah was the first Saudi king ever to visit China since the establishment of diplomatic relations between the two countries in 1990. China's state-run news agency, Xinhua, naturally emphasized the significance of the trip and the rapid rate of growth in the trade and investment relations between the two countries, focused on the energy sector.

During the summer of 2006, after Israel's war on Lebanon's Hezbollah movement, which led to the destruction of much of Lebabon's insfrastructure, King Abdullah voiced Saudi Arabia's readiness to provide Lebanon with financial support to rebuild the country, demonstrating that under King Abdullah, Saudi

Arabia has indeed adopted a far more assertive role to bring peace to the Middle East. This was also on display in the Mecca Accords hosted by Abdullah in February 2007. Hosting the leaders of the two main Palestinian political factions—the Fattah-backed President Mahmoud Abbas and the Hamas leader Khaled Meshaal—Saudi Arabia played the lead role in promoting the creation a Palestinian national unity government. During the same month, Saudi Arabia hosted Russian President Vladimir Putin and voiced its readiness to help the cause of peace in the Middle East.

Saudi Arabia's new assertive policy in the Middle East was also vividly on display in late March 2007. Coinciding with Iran's capture of "trespassing" British mariners in the Persian Gulf, King Abdullah dropped the gauntlet. At the Arab summit convened in Riyadh, Abdullah became the first Arab monarch to call the American and British occupation of Iraq "illegal." A feature-length interview with Foreign Minister Saud al-Faisal, published in *Newsweek*,[5] was titled "Saudi's War of Independence from Washington." The following passages from the interview are very telling. In response to a question on why Saudi Arabia has suddenly moved to the forefront of diplomatic action in the region, ("Because of Iraq? The Palestinian Issue? Lebanon? Iran?") Saud al-Faisal replied:

It's all these things together—the feeling that in the Arab world things are happening as if there are no people in the region who have their own separate will, that there are no people in the region who can protect their own interests, or even their own territory . . . [infighting among Palestinians] created in the King a feeling that disaster was going to happen in the Arab world; that unless we grasp our fate in our hands and move to resolve our own problems, we're going to be just a people that once were there—and are no longer there.

On the specific issue of Saudi-Iranian relations, Saud al-Faisal said,

We told [the Iranians] that their interference in Arab affairs is creating a backlash in the Arab world and in the Muslim world . . . But we have never put ourselves in a position of conflict with Iran.

The impact of the evolving rapprochement between Iran and Saudi Arabia is indeed vast. The most immediate effect on Iran is to make Iranian leaders acknowledge that they cannot be more Arab than Arabs themselves, and that they should cede to Saudi Arabia and other Arab countries the responsibility for supporting the Palestinians and Lebanese. In the absence of a strong Saudi presence, this could not have been an option. With Saudi Arabia's newly assertive policy in the region, however, given the vast wealth at the kingdom's disposal, Iran seems convinced that interference in Arab affairs will harm its relations not only with Saudi Arabia and its GCC allies, but with the Arab world more broadly. It is indeed unnatural for Iran—as a non-Arab country—to champion the Arab cause more than the Arabs themselves. Untangling itself from Arab-Israeli disputes is indeed one of the most promising aspects of Iran's evolving foreign policy.

From the Saudi perspective, improved relations with Iran have the benefit of showing the Saudi people and other Arabs that the Saudi Royal Family are indeed independent and legitimate actors who make their own decisions based on their own national interests, and that they will not blindly follow the United States or any other country. At the same time, cooperating with Iran, OPEC's second largest oil producer, will allow the Saudis to maintain their leadership position in OPEC. In the above-noted *Newsweek* interview, when asked if Saudi Arabia would consider forcing oil prices down to punish Iran (as Saudi Arabia had done in the 1980s), Saud al-Faisal's response was a categorical "No. People need oil."

Another significant impact of Iranian-Saudi relations is Iran's evolving relations with the GCC. Since the GCC was created as a mechanism to counter Iran, the improvement of Iran's relationship with Saudi Arabia will allay other Persian Gulf countries' anxieties about Iranian adventurism in their countries. It will also lessen the GCC's need for relying on the United States and the UK for their security. The forward and massive presence of foreign military forces in the Persian Gulf works to delegitimize pro-Western monarchs in the region before their people. Since any instability among the Arab monarchies will harm American and British interests in the area, it seems as though Iran, the GCC, as well as the United States and the UK have a common interest in supporting the evolving rapprochement between Iran and its former adversaries in the GCC.

RELATIONS WITH RUSSIA

Ever since the then Parliament Speaker Rafsanjani's trip to Moscow in 1989, where he was received by the then president Mikael Gorbachev, Iran has counted on Russia as a strategic partner. During the two-term presidency of Rafsanjani (1989–1997), Iran became Russia's largest trading partner in the Middle East, and its main ally in the region. In the 1990s, Russian arms sales to Iran allowed the latter to refurbish its badly depleted military infrastructure. To be sure, during the Iran-Iraq war, the Soviet Union had been Iraq's leading supplier of arms. Yet after Saddam Hussein's invasion of Kuwait and the dissolution of the Soviet Union, in 1990 and 1991 respectively, Iran and Russia's importance to each other rose exponentially.

For the first time in their modern history beginning in the 1990s, Moscow and Tehran no longer shared land borders with one another. This automatically removed a major source of tension between them. The dissolution of the Soviet Union meant that instead of the Soviet behemoth, Iran now had borders with three small, relatively weak former Soviet republics: Azerbaijan, Armenia, and Turkmenistan, none of whom were capable of threatening Iran's territorial integrity the way tsarist Russia and the Soviet Union had. Despite this fact, however, throughout the 1990s, Iran did not succeed in significantly expanding its influence among its new neighbors. Stiff American opposition to the northward expansion of Iranian influence among the newly independent countries paralyzed Iran's efforts to gain solid footholds in the Caucasus and Central Asia. In fact, U.S. policy in the 1990s rested on driving a wedge between the newly independent countries of the Caucasus and Central Asia on the one hand, and Russia and Iran on the other. This alone was enough to drive Russia and Iran into each other's arms. In the early 1990s, as American and British oil companies worked on deepening their foothold in the Caspian Sea region, Iran was not allowed to join any of the oil consortia that were created under American and European leadership in the area. The most significant blow to Iran was the blocking of its bid to join the Azerbaijan International Operating Company, which was led by British Petroleum. Similarly, throughout the 1990s, the United States was the main opponent of oil swap arrangements between Iran and Kazakhstan.

Upon assuming Russia's presidency in the year 2000, Vladimir Putin built on the already strong Russian-Iranian relationship, which had been developed under his predecessor, Boris Yeltsin. Under Yeltsin Russia had signed major arms sales agreements with Iran, providing the latter with fighter jets, submarines, and tanks. In the late 1990s, Russia had also begun work on Iran's main nuclear reactor at the Persian Gulf port of Bushehr. Under Yeltsin, the two countries had cooperated on Central Asian issues, especially so in the case of containing instability in Tajikistan and Afghanistan, both of which have Persian-speaking majorities. During the first Russian campaign in Chechnya in 1994–1996, Iran had overlooked Russia's harsh suppression of Muslim militants who fought for secession from Moscow in Russia's southernmost region in the Caucasus.

Putin's presidency has seen a further deepening of Russian-Iranian relations. Soon after assuming office, Putin abrogated Russia's promises outlined in the Gore-Chernomyrdin agreement, under which Russia had agreed to cease selling arms to Iran by the year 2000. As Russia sought to reconstitute its position as a leading power in the greater Middle East, it became Iran's key supporter against attempts by the United States and, to a lesser extent, the EU, to isolate Iran.

The impracticality of the U.S. policy of isolating the new countries of the Caucasus and Central Asia from their southern *and* northern neighbors became evident at the end of the 1990s. With the creation of SCO, which we discussed previously, and with Russia's resurgence as a major power, the United States came to be seen as a source of tension and instability in the former Soviet south. While the Yeltsin years were times of decline for and disintegration in Russia, Putin has succeeded in reviving Russia's significant role in international relations. While Yeltsin had followed Washington's line, Putin, in sharp contrast, has been one of the harshest critics of American foreign policy, especially during the second term of President George W. Bush.

Putin's most stinging criticism of U.S. unilateralism and militarism was aired in his speech to the annual Munich Security Conference in February 2007, after which the Russian president embarked on an unprecedented trip to Saudi Arabia. At Munich, Putin was harshly critical of any attempt at forcing an American-led "unipolar world" into existence." He declared,

Today we are witnessing an almost uncontained hyper use of force—military force—in international relations, force that is plunging the world into an abyss of permanent conflicts. As a result we do not have sufficient strength to find a comprehensive solution to any one of these conflicts. Finding a political settlement also becomes impossible. We are seeing a greater and greater disdain for the basic principles of international law. And independent legal norms are, as a matter of fact, coming increasingly closer to one state's legal system. One state and, of course, first and foremost the United States, has overstepped its national borders in every way. This is visible in the economic, political, cultural and educational policies it imposes on other nations. Well, who likes this? Who is happy about this? ... In international relations we increasingly see the desire to resolve a given question according to so-called issues of political expediency, based on the current political climate. And of course this is extremely dangerous. It results in the fact that no one feels safe. I want to emphasize this—no one feels safe! Because no one can feel that international law is like a stone wall that will protect them. Of course such a policy stimulates an arms race.

The force's dominance inevitably encourages a number of countries to acquire weapons of mass destruction. Moreover, significantly new threats—though they were also well-known before—have appeared, and today threats such as terrorism have taken on a global character. I am convinced that we have reached that decisive moment when we must seriously think about the architecture of global security.

And we must proceed by searching for a reasonable balance between the interests of all participants in the international dialogue. Especially since the international landscape is so varied and changes so quickly—changes in light of the dynamic development in a whole number of countries and regions. Madam Federal Chancellor already mentioned this. The combined GDP measured in purchasing power parity of countries such as India and China is already greater than that of the United States. And a similar calculation with the GDP of the BRIC countries—Brazil, Russia, India and China—surpasses the cumulative GDP of the EU. And according to experts this gap will only increase in the future.

There is no reason to doubt that the economic potential of the new centres of global economic growth will inevitably be converted into political influence and will strengthen multipolarity.[6]

Never in the post–Cold War era had the leader of a major power offered such a blunt criticism of U.S. foreign policy. Putin's remarks were so critical of the United States that the highest-ranking American participant to the Munich Security Conference, Defense Secretary Robert Gates, was compelled to say that it reminded him of the Cold War era!

For a country like Iran, which has been subjected to U.S. sanctions and threats of force for close to thirty years, it is natural that Putin's remarks are viewed with sympathy. To be sure, a close scrutiny of Ahmadinejad's two letters to America, especially the one he wrote to President Bush, shows that they are strikingly similar to Putin's remarks on America's role in the world—the main difference being Ahmadinejad's constant reference to religious and otherworldly matters, while Putin's is solidly anchored in the discourse of contemporary international relations.

In the current regional and international environment, Iran and Russia have at least three significant areas of mutual interest: ensuring stability in the still-fledgling countries of Central Asia and the Caucasus, preventing the spread of religious extremism, and the possible creation of a natural gas cartel, or a "gas OPEC."[7]

Given the significant expansion of Russia's economic and security ties with China, and with its expanding economic links to the EU, Russia's interest in maintaining a forward position in the Caucasus and Central Asia has lessened. In Moscow's current calculations, its relations with the republics of the former Soviet South are far less significant than its relations with Europe and China. It stands to reason, therefore, that continuing cooperation with Russia will enable Iran to be more active than it has been so far in its trade, investment, and security ties with Armenia, Azerbaijan, and Turkmenistan, as well as with Afghanistan and Tajikistan. While U.S. policy has traditionally aimed to weaken Iran's ties to its neighbors, it is clear by now that such an inflexible American focus on containing Iran has held the whole region back, while undermining the stability of a vitally important part of the world.

In a more normal geopolitical environment, in cooperation with Russia and the United States, Iran possesses the capacity to meet the growing economic and security needs of newly independent republics of the former Soviet Union in the Caucasus and Central Asia. In the case of a few such countries, especially Azerbaijan, Turkmenistan, Afghanistan, and Tajikistan, the common cultural and linguistic ties that they share with Iran can be utilized for the benefit of all. As we discussed in the previous chapter while exploring the idea of a "Turko-Persian Realm," given the gas shortages from Russia that have affected Georgia and Armenia, among other countries, these countries have officially expressed their interest in receiving Iranian gas exports. At the same time, according to the Russian daily *Kommersant*, an agreement is in the making for the creation of a natural gas cartel.[8] Such a consortium would include Russia, Iran, Qatar, Venezuela, and Algeria, which together possess over 70 percent of the world's natural gas reserves.

The idea of an international gas consortium was first proposed by President Putin in 2002. Iran, which possesses 15 percent of the world's natural gas—second only to Russia—would be a highly significant player in any attempt at creating such a cartel. Iran's significance goes far beyond the gas it possesses and is tied to the country's location. Numerous hungry markets to Iran's northwest through Turkey, and to Iran's east, especially Pakistan and India, would benefit tremendously from a steady supply of gas from Iran. In the absence of a consortium to coordinate their policies, the supply of gas to expanding international markets would be far less reliable. Just as oil-exporting countries have an interest in cooperating with one another, so, too, gas rich countries have an interest in steady markets and reasonable prices. To be sure, the politics and geopolitics of gas are different from oil in significant ways. The most important difference is the fact that the interruption of piped gas from one source cannot be as easily redressed as in the oil markets. Once major pipelines are in place to connect suppliers and consumers, the interdependence between them is far more stable than is the case in the oil markets.

Despite numerous areas of common interest between them, a potential area of contention between Russia and Iran is the division of the Caspian Sea. During Soviet times, Iran had access to less than one-tenth of the Caspian sea as it faced a far stronger neighbor to its north. After the unraveling of the Soviet Union, there was hope that Iran could get a fairer share of the sea, but with Russia and the United States opposed to Iran's expanded navigation, fishing, and oil exploration rights, Iran has largely remained as ineffective in this area as it was during the Soviet Union's existence. Since Russia is Iran premier source of modern weapons, including naval equipment, Iran is obviously in no position to challenge Russia militarily in the Caspian. However, since Iran is Russia's largest market in the Middle East, Iran may tie some of its future purchases of Russian equipment to more extensive rights in the Caspian region. While Russia cooperated with the Western-led consortia that have habitually excluded Iran, this policy would have to be modified if Russian-Iranian relations are to remain on the solid footing of the past seventeen years.

Another area of contention between Russia and Iran has to do with their nuclear cooperation. While Iran has paid Russia hundreds of millions of dollars in the past decade to complete the nuclear reactor in Bushehr, under U.S. and European pressure Moscow has continuously delayed the completion of the reactor, using the excuse that Iran has fallen behind on its payments, or technical issues of incompatibility with the original German design of the reactor. Initially, beginning in the 1990s, Russia was supposed to complete the reactor by the year 2000; then the completion date was pushed back to 2003, 2004, 2005, 2006, and now, in mid-2007, it seems unlikely that Russia will fulfill its promises before the end of the current decade. Russia's reneging on its promises to Iran should demonstrate to Iranian leaders the price the country is paying because of its international isolation, which has placed Iran in a position of utter weakness vis-à-vis Russia.

From a Russian standpoint, it is natural that the country will not sacrifice its more important relationship with the United States and especially with Europe to meet Iran's demands. For Iran, the only way to ensure more reliable Russian service is to break out of its current isolation from the world's most advanced countries, and to improve its relations with Europe and the United States. More broadly, Iran must allay the anxieties of the world's main powers about its nuclear program, which has led to successive United Nations Security Council resolutions against the country. While Iran had hoped that Russia and China would oppose the United States and its European allies in their attempt to impose a nuclear quarantine on Iran, both of these countries have, understandably, sided with the world's main powers. The current Iranian government simply lacks the international credibility to expect seamless cooperation from Russia, China, India, or other countries that are capable of helping Iran's nuclear program.

RELATIONS WITH INDIA

One of the most promising developments in Iranian foreign policy is the country's expanding relationship with India. Beginning in the mid-1990s, New Delhi began seeing Iran as the key link to expanding India's reach in Central Asia and the Persian Gulf regions. In the final two years of Rafsanjani's tenure as Iran's president, the two countries reached a significant naval cooperation agreement, wherein the Indian navy helped Iran modify the batteries of its Russian-built diesel submarines to adapt to the warm water conditions of the Persian Gulf region. Since that time, Iran's ties to India have grown rapidly and show no signs of slowing down. India is far more advanced than Iran in industrial, technological, and military know-how, while Iran is ideally positioned to provide a growing share of India's burgeoning need for imported oil and gas, and to act as a bridge for India to the Persian Gulf and Caspian Sea-Central Asia regions, and to serve, along with Pakistan, as a goodwill ambassador between India and the Muslim world.

Iran's exploration of military cooperation with India dates back to the time of Mohammad Reza Shah. In the early winter of 1978, the commander of the Iranian army, General Gholamali Oveissi, accompanied by a high-ranking military delegation, paid a two-week visit to India, where the two countries explored avenues for expanded cooperation. At that time Iran, as the main U.S. ally in the Persian Gulf region, had access to some of the most advanced American military hardware, while India relied on Soviet technology to refurbish its armed forces. The largest obstacle to the development of bilateral relations during the Shah's time was that the two countries belonged to opposite camps. Iran's membership in the Central Treaty Organization (CENTO) bound it to Pakistan, which was also a member of the pact. In the 1965 and 1971 wars between India and Pakistan, Iran provided political as well as nominal military assistance to Pakistan.[9]

Throughout the 1970s, as the Shah crafted a more balanced foreign policy for Iran, positioning it in between east and west, a thaw came about in relations between the two countries. After the revolution, relations with India improved steadily. A milestone in bilateral relations was reached in 1993, when Indian Prime Minister Narasimha Rao became the first Indian leader to pay an official visit to postrevolutionary Iran. That trip was termed a "turning point" by Rafsanjani. Two years later, in 1995, Rafsanjani made a reciprocal visit to India. Then, in 2001, Indian Prime Minister Atal Bihari Vajpayee visited Tehran, where he and his host President Mohammad Khatami signed the "Tehran Declaration," which amounted to a comprehensive agreement in a variety of areas, including defense cooperation.

Two years later, in January 2003, President Khatami made a state visit to Delhi, where he was the guest of honor at India's Independence Day celebrations, a privilege rarely accorded by Indian leaders to foreign heads of state. The "New Delhi Declaration" signed during Khatami's visit further expanded cooperation between the two countries, with a focus on defense cooperation. The declaration came with seven Memoranda of Understanding between the two countries, including expanded cooperation in information technology, food technology, and pharmaceuticals. The key area of focus was India-Iran cooperation in combating international terrorism, and the common stance of the two countries that the tension between the United States and Iraq should be solved through the UN, and not through unilateral military action.

In the past decade, coinciding with its rapid economic growth and technological advancement, India has increasingly seen its role in global terms. It has sought to expand its influence and strategic reach beyond South Asia. One of the most important areas for India has been Central Asia, including Afghanistan, and the Middle East. Iran is capable of acting as a bridge between India and these regions. A significant reason for India's interest in the Central Asia and Middle East regions is these regions' vast oil and gas reserves, which are essential for India's economic growth. As the world's sixth largest consumer of energy, India relies on imports for about 75 percent of its total oil and gas consumption. With current oil imports of over 2 million barrels a day, if current trends continue, India is on the path to becoming an even larger energy importer. It is estimated that by 2020 India is likely to trail only the United States, China, and Japan in this area. In terms of its potential to meet India's rapidly growing need for energy imports, Iran figures very prominently in Indian thinking. Nowhere is this more significant than in the proposed gas pipeline that is supposed to carry Iranian natural gas to Pakistan and on to India and, at a later stage, to China. Iran is indeed the most economical and reliable source of energy for India. Yet, over the past decade, U.S. opposition to the construction of oil and gas pipelines through Iran and, more broadly, to the development of Iran's energy sector, has been a major obstacle in this area of mutual interest between India and Iran.

Two relatively new developments have made the prospect for the building of the Iran-Pakistan-India pipeline brighter than it has ever been. One is the steady change that has appeared on this topic in the thinking of government-affiliated analysts within the United States over the past year. The above-quoted essay by Christine Fair, and another scholarly essay by Kenneth Katzman and Alan Kronstadt argue that the United States should in fact support the expansion of Indo-Iranian relations, and the construction of the Iran-Pakistan-India gas pipeline.[10] This thinking has also been reflected in the remarks of Secretary of State Condoleezza Rice to the U.S. Senate Foreign Relations Committee on April 5, 2006. At that hearing, Senator Lincoln Chaffee asked whether increasing U.S.-India nuclear cooperation could guarantee that the proposed Iran-India gas pipeline would not be built. In response, Secretary Rice noted:

> Well, I can't be assured that it will not. But let me just note that India is of course not the only country with an oil and gas relationship with Iran. Some of our closest allies—Japan—has an oil and gas relationship with Iran. [Among] the Europeans, Italy is Iran's largest trading partner. So, most countries have a different relationship with Iran than we do.

The other development that augurs well for the pipeline's prospects is the increasingly assertive statements of Indian and Pakistani officials on their independence from the United States on this issue. In August 2005, Indian Prime Minister Manmohan Singh said to India's Parliament that "[t]he United States has no influence over the fate of Iran-Pakistan-India gas pipeline."[11] Singh claimed that neither he nor any U.S. officials had brought up any opposition to pipeline's construction during his state visit to the United States in the early summer of 2005. Singh added, "I only referred to the issue in an interview with the *Washington Post* there, stating that India is in dire need of Iran's gas to meet its rising energy shortcomings." Also, "We enjoy excellent historic ties with Iran and India has the largest population of Shi'as among all countries in the world, next to Iran."[12]

While discussions between Iran, Pakistan, and India on the construction of the 2,600-kilometer gas pipeline have continued since the mid-1990s, a series of disputes between India and Pakistan on the one hand, and between Iran and the United States on the other, have delayed the start of construction. Increasingly, however, the project is seen by Iran, Pakistan, and India as a "peace pipeline," that can boost interdependence among all three countries, especially between Pakistan and India. In the case of Pakistan, the country can also expect to earn substantial transit fees, while benefiting from a reliable and clean source of energy from a neighboring supplier. Similarly, India's economic development and environmental protection will receive a strong boost once the pipeline is complete. Given the estimated $7 billion price tag for the project, however, the technical and financial support of the world's leading countries is indispensable.

RELATIONS WITH CHINA

Of Iran's new partners among the world's major powers, China holds the preeminent position. China is currently Iran's leading trading partner, with two-way trade reaching over $12 billion in 2006. In the preceding decade, two-way trade between the two countries had risen more than tenfold, which marks the steepest expansion Iran has experienced in its trade relations in the postrevolutionary period. The rapid expansion of economic relations between the two countries has corresponded to a deepening of Tehran's security relations with Peking. Iran relies on China for a vast array of consumer and industrial goods, and for the development of the country's transportation infrastructure.

One of the most significant areas of cooperation between the two countries has been the Chinese-led completion of Tehran's metro, which was accomplished in the late 1990s. Currently, Chinese engineers and construction firms are laying the groundwork for an ambitious project to build a freeway from Tehran to the Caspian coast, which will cut through the high altitudes of the Alborz. Along with the Tehran metro project, the Tehran-Caspian freeway is the most ambitious construction project in Iran since the revolution.

Since the mid-1990s, China and Iran have expanded their cooperation in fields ranging from oil and gas and nuclear research to tourism and a broad array of industrial joint ventures. In the new century, especially, with the rise of the Chinese-led Shanghai Cooperation Organization, Sino-Iranian relations have been bolstered by a shared suspicion of U.S. plans in the regions that surround the two countries. China's ever-growing thirst for fossil fuels, and Iran's desire to become a more significant power in the Persian Gulf and Caspian Sea regions, have solidified the common interests between them. To be sure, China's relations with other oil-rich countries have also expanded and include new openings to Saudi Arabia. Yet Iran remains China's main economic partner in the Middle East. Following the dissolution of the Soviet Union, China, similar to India, also sees Iran as a bridge to the Caspian Sea region, which is rich in oil and gas reserves, and an arena of strategic rivalry among the world's great powers.

Akbar Hashemi Rafsanjani's two trips to China, first as the Iranian parliament's speaker in 1985, and then during his presidency in 1992, opened to door to expanded relations between the two countries. In 1989, when he served as Iran's president, Seyed Ali Khamenei had become the first Iranian chief executive to visit China. These contacts reached a high point in June 2000, when the then president Mohammad Khatami paid a four-day visit to China. The China-Iran Joint Communiqué signed between Khatami and the then Chinese President Jiang Zemin was a milestone in bilateral relations. The following statements in the communiqué demonstrate the core of shared perspectives between the two countries. What stands out in the communiqué is the shared strategic vision of both sides in expanding ties in all fields, and their common interest in promoting "multipolarization," and opposing "hegemonism," which were thinly veiled references to the United States[13]:

[The two presidents] reached common understanding on enhancing bilateral cooperation, opening up new prospects for the bilateral ties and establishing a 21st century-oriented long-term and wide-ranging relationship of friendship and cooperation in the strategic interests of the two countries on the basis of mutual respect for sovereignty and territorial integrity, equality and mutual benefit, and peaceful co-existence.

The two sides agreed to strengthen cooperation in energy, transportation, telecommunications, science, technology, industry, banking, tourism, agriculture, mining, environmental protection and other fields, and encourage the relevant companies of the two countries to explore the possibilities of further cooperation in the field of petroleum and natural gas ... The two sides maintained that the Silk Road had laid a solid foundation for cultural exchanges between the ancient civilizations of China and Iran in east and west of Asia, and that the revitalization of the Silk Road would contribute significantly to the consolidation and development of the cultural, art, tourist and people-to-people exchanges and contacts between the two peoples.

Both sides stand for world multipolarization. They stressed the need to establish an equitable, just, fair and reasonable new international political and economic order that is free of hegemonism and power politics and is based on equality. They indicated their readiness to work together for the establishment of such a new order.

The two sides underscored the importance of establishing an international community for cooperation, participation and dialogue and against the use or threat of force and imposition of economic sanctions to settle disputes between countries. The two sides support the important role played by the UN in safeguarding world peace and security and in helping developing countries raise their development level. The two sides stressed the importance of adhering to the principles and purposes of the UN Charter.

In April 2002, Jiang Zemin became the first Chinese President in history to pay an official visit to Iran. His visit, during which he met with numerous Iranian political leaders, further solidified the areas of mutual interest outlined in the communiqué. As the communiqué made clear, the increasing closeness of the Sino-Iranian relationship must be viewed in historical and contemporary terms. China and Iran have rich cultural and national identities, and see themselves and each other as proud, ancient civilizations. Since China has no colonial or imperialist record in its dealings with Iran, there are no historical grievances between them. Postrevolutionary Iran has maintained its "anti-imperialist" outlook, and has responded to U.S. attempts at containing it by backing anti-U.S. groups in the region. In this context, Iran has come to see China as an effective counterweight to the United States in Iran and the region that surrounds it. Despite the incompatibility of Islam and communism as the two countries' respective state ideologies, both countries have consistently chosen cool-headed pragmatism over ideological rigidity. Nowhere has this been more evident than in Iran's reluctance to offer even rhetorical support to the restive Muslim Uigurs in China's northwestern Xinjiang region. Similar to Iran's pragmatic stance on Russia's treatment of Muslims in Chechnya, Iran has steadily seen its relationship with China as far more important than Muslim unity or other ideological causes. While in the 1980s Khomeini had made critical comments about "God-less" communism, few traces of this thinking can be found in Iran's foreign policy thinking in the post-Khomeini era, especially in Sino-Iranian relations.

Peking's history of providing a range of weapons to Iran, including missile technology, which dates back to the Iran-Iraq war, have alarmed the United States and some of its allies.

The alliance between Iran and China has shown the supremacy of geopolitical thinking over ideology and religious fervor. While China sold weapons to Iraq and Iran concurrently during the 1980s, it was the only major country that supplied arms to Iran. The main Arab countries, including Saudi Arabia and Egypt, as well as major powers including the United States, numerous European countries, and the Soviet Union had almost entirely supported Iraq during that war. In contrast to India's passive role, China became the only supplier of advanced antiship and long-range missile technology to Iran at a time when Iran needed such supplies most.

After the establishment of diplomatic relations between China and Iran in 1971, the two countries began seeing each other in nonideological terms. While the Shah's government suppressed Iran's communist movement, Beijing chose to overlook this fact and focused instead on areas of strategic convergence, which included the two countries' shared suspicions of Soviet hegemony. Beginning in the 1960s, as Moscow and Peking drifted apart, the Shah saw Peking as a powerful partner, and independent of the two superpowers of the Cold War. Despite this fact, however, since Iran was firmly anchored in the Western camp, relations remained limited throughout the 1970s. It was the Iranian revolution of 1979 that wrought a sea change in the relationship. The clerical system's antipathy toward Washington and Moscow throughout the 1980s, which was vividly on display during the Iran-Iraq war, created a major opening in bilateral relations.

Throughout the 1980s, Peking supported Iran's drift to strategic nonalignment. On the whole, China supported Iran's antagonism toward Iraq, a nation that Beijing had seen as a Soviet proxy. When the war ended, Peking officially announced that it wished to assist in Iran's reconstruction drive at a time when war-devastated Iran had no other allies among the world's major powers.

In the 1990s, Iran consistently turned to China for refurbishing its degraded military infrastructure. Second only to Russia as a source of weapons for Iran, China also increased its assistance to Iran's nuclear program. In 1992 the two countries signed an unprecedented nuclear cooperation agreement. While consistent U.S. pressure on China succeeded in limiting nuclear cooperation between it and Iran, it did not manage to completely halt this cooperation. Another milestone was reached in 1993, when the two countries created the Chinese-Iranian Joint Commission on Economic, Trade, Scientific, and Technical Cooperation. That was also the year in which China became, for the first time in its history, a net importer of oil, thus becoming fundamentally dependent on oil imports from the Persian Gulf region, where Iran quickly became a reliable source of oil for China. In 1996, following the passage of extraterritorial, secondary sanctions by the United States against Iran, enshrined in the Iran-Libya Sanctions Act, China continued its independent policy toward Iran and refused to bow to U.S. demands to isolate Iran. China's reliability became another pillar in the steady expansion of ties between the two countries in the 1990s and after.

Given China's rapidly growing energy needs, and Iran's continuing isolation from Western countries, Sino-Iranian relations seem destined to grow further in the years ahead. Current figures show that China imports about 60 percent of its oil needs; by 2020, that figure is expected to rise to over 75 percent. While Iran currently supplies China with about 15 percent of the latter's oil imports, with the entry of gas into the equation and expansion of Iran's LNG (Liquified Natural Gas) exports to China, Iran is destined to figure even more prominently in China's energy security calculations. Given the fact that Persian Gulf producers are collectively the largest source of energy imports for China, Iran's prominent geopolitical position in the area enables it to act as a guarantor of reliable energy shipments to China into the future. China's energy ties to Saudi Arabia have also grown precipitously in the past decade, which shows the long-term strategic thinking of Chinese leaders in their ties to the Persian Gulf region. What makes Iran's position especially valuable to China is that Iran also borders the energy-rich Caspian Sea region, in which China has made massive investments.

Iran's position among the main energy exporters improved noticeably in 2003, when Iranian officials announced that the Azadegan oil field, located in southwestern Iran, would potentially increase the country's crude oil reserves by close to 40 billion barrels. This discovery boosted Iran's oil reserves to over 130 billion barrels, which amounts to over 11 percent of the world's total oil reserves, second only to Saudi Arabia. Given the fact that Iran also possesses the world's second largest natural gas reserves (behind only Russia), it is natural that the fuel-thirsty economies of China and India have crafted energy relationships with Iran that are independent of American and European demands. This is especially the case at present, when China and India have become more sensitive to environmental hazards of pollution-causing fuels, especially coal and gasoline.

The year 2004 was especially important for Iran-China energy cooperation. China's state-run SINOPEC agreed to purchase LNG from Iran for twenty-five years, in a deal that is worth more than $100 billion. This will be based on China receiving 250 million tons of Iranian LNG over the next two decades. In 2004 SINOPEC also signed a major oil exploration and transport deal with Iran to develop Iran's Yadavaran oil field, from which China is slated to receive 150,000 barrels of oil a day for the next two decades. This is likely to increase Iran's share in China's oil imports from the current level of 15 percent. As noted above, China is already the leading purchaser of Iranian oil and the leading investor in Iran's energy sector.

China has significant security concerns in the Persian Gulf because of its energy dependence on the region. In the case of new conflicts in the Persian Gulf, which could disrupt oil that is destined for China, China would encounter significant bottlenecks. Thus, China has invested significantly in diversifying its energy sources, with significant investments in Angola and Sudan, and in building oil and gas pipelines from the Caspian region to China. Among the most significant of these is China's leadership in building a 1,000-kilometer oil pipeline from Kazakhstan to western China, and also in connecting Kazakhstan's pipelines to the Iranian network. China has also officially expressed its interest in building gas pipelines from Turkmenistan to its domestic markets. Given its strategic geographic location, Iran is directly affected by China's growing energy interests in the Persian Gulf and Caspian Sea regions.

While trade and investment in energy projects constitutes the largest sector in the growing economic relationship between China and Iran, other areas of mutual interest are on the rise as well. In the spring of 2005, Chinese and Iranian aerospace officials met in Beijing to explore cooperation in this sector. Furthermore, in the summer of 2005, a senior Iranian delegation traveled to China to explore ways in which China can help Iran become a member of the World Trade Organization. Another key area of mutual interest between the two countries is China's lead role in building a billion-dollar aluminum smelter in the Persian Gulf port of Bandar Abbas. Finally, given the history of cooperation between the two countries in the nuclear field, if Russian-Iranian cooperation continues to face obstacles, especially vis-à-vis the completion of the Bushehr reactor, it is possible that Iran will attempt to replace Russia with China and/or India in this area.

While the pillars of Iran's current relations with China and India were laid during Mohammad Reza Shah's time in the 1960s and 1970s, two key factors have made these two countries more important to Iran's current calculations than they have ever been. The first is that postrevolutionary Iran has seen its place in the world in anti-imperialist terms. Since, traditionally, China and India have also dealt with Western powers from a position of weakness, the three countries have shown a common interest in redressing what they see as the global imbalance of wealth and power. Second, for the first time in over two centuries, China and India are dealing with Western countries from a position of independence and parity. This is one reason they have not followed European or American prescriptions to downgrade or sever their ties to Iran.

The challenge for Iranian foreign policymakers, as we saw in the previous chapter, is to build Iran up as a bridge between East and West, not as the exclusive domain of any of the world's individual power blocks. In the absence of significant American and European demand for Iran's goods and services, Iran is likely to be placed at the mercy of its Asian partners, especially Russia, India, and China, which are far more advanced and powerful than Iran in economic, technological, and military spheres. While China and India are especially important partners for Iran's future development, Iranian leaders must realize—as they have after the passage of United Nations Security Council Resolution number 1737 in late March 2007—that Iran's Asian partners, while independent from Europe and the United States, will not sacrifice their far more substantial dealings with the major Western powers over Iran. In that sense, Iran's exclusive reliance on its Asian partners to protect its interests in the international arena are unrealistic. Iran would be better off learning from the adroit and sophisticated international relations of Peking and New Delhi. While China and India possess the economic and military wherewithal to compete with, and even oppose, Western demands, they take great care never to call Europe or America their opponents. It is indeed ironic that Iran, among whose main nonenergy exports are carpets, dried fruits, and pistachio nuts, officially calls Western countries its opponents, and even its enemies. One of the main promises of Iranian foreign policy in the next decade is to overcome such unrealistic posturing and to actually learn from India and China's examples. Continuously referring to the "divine" system of the Islamic Republic and relying on the afterlife for salvation are not becoming of statesmen and stateswomen in the early twenty-first century. The sooner Iranian leaders learn this, the better off their country will be.

CHAPTER FOUR

Pathways to Development: The Search for Stable Progress

Since Mahmoud Ahmadinejad's election to Iran's presidency in 2005, coverage of Iran by the world's media has almost exclusively focused on the country's dispute with the international community over its nuclear program, and on the shocking rhetoric of the Iranian president. What the extensive media coverage of Iran has rarely addressed is that, for the vast majority of Iran's 70 million people, the most pressing concerns are not their country's ability to enrich uranium, nor its policy toward Iraq and the Arab-Israeli dispute. The main focus of Iranians is making ends meet, and building better, more prosperous lives for themselves and their children. Far more pressing for Iranians than championing the cause of Palestine, exporting Islamic revolution, and promoting global justice is embarking on multifaceted and sustainable development in their national life, including the cultural, political, and, especially, economic spheres. The lingering otherworldly declarations of Iranian leaders, replete with references to God, the prophets, and the benefits of martyrdom, have only perpetuated the image of Iranians as an irrational and unreasonable people, giving the false impression that Iranians and their leaders are less interested in jobs, public welfare, and developing their country than they are in clinging to their rigid ideological positions.

Ahmadinejad's election to the presidency was attributable, at least in part, to his embrace of economic populism and his promise to bring the country's oil wealth directly to the population. During the presidential election of June 2005, Iran's state television interviewed Ahmadinejad, who had served for the preceding three years as Tehran's mayor, in his modest home in a working-class neighborhood of Tehran. This portrayal of Ahmadinejad's simple lifestyle was immediately cast in sharp contrast to other Iranian leaders who had grown rich while holding public office. The interviewer asked Ahmadinejad's son, "where is your sauna?" The response was a quick, "we have no sauna." The interview helped solidify Ahmadinejad's image as an honest man of the people who was not after personal gain. For the Iranian electorate, who had seen their standards of living dwindle while witnessing the amassing of large fortunes by the country's political elite, Ahmadinejad's modest means and his seeming rectitude became his most important credentials.[1]

Once in office, Ahmadinejad embraced economic populism and focused on social justice issues, presenting himself, in the words of a Wall Street Journal reporter, "as an Iranian version of Venezuela's Hugo Chavez."[2] Early in his presidency, Ahmadinejad proposed billions of dollars for a national school renovation program, and moved to raise the salaries of government employees and the minimum wage, and doubled the amount of government grants to newlyweds. While these policies added to Ahmadinejad's popularity within Iran, they have also raised concerns about artificially raising expectations, which will be hard to meet. Record oil prices, which have made the government's coffers swell, have indeed begun to trickle down to the population. But can the policy of dealing with the symptoms of poverty be effective in addressing its root causes as well? While Iran had made tentative steps toward liberalizing its economy during Khatami's presidency, Ahmadinejad's reversion to an Islamic socialism is unlikely to be sustainable. Iran simply lacks the resources to offer generous subsidies to its burgeoning population. The only way to improve the people's condition in the long term is to invest in the productive capacity of Iranians, and to create an environment where the private sector feels secure enough to innovate and create long-term employment. The economic problems of Iran run deep. With double-digit levels of inflation and unemployment, the oil revenues of the country must be utilized to enhance the nation's productive capacity by refurbishing the country's infrastructure and by investing in productive enterprises. Iran's economic problems cannot be addressed overnight, and certainly not through relying on short-term handouts. Over the past few years, the annual amount that the government spends on subsidizing basic necessities and consumer goods, such as bread, rice, sugar, cheese, cooking oil, and fuels, especially heating oil, gas, and gasoline, has topped $20 billion per year. The government relied on its oil revenues, which topped $50 billion in 2006, to finance its budget shortfalls. What Iranian leaders are careful never to ask is, What will happen when oil revenues decline and the government is forced to scale back its subsidies?

Iranians, similar to citizens of other countries, seek hope in their future. Yet it seems that such a future has not been portrayed in any significant detail by the country's leadership. Iranian leaders rarely discuss the country's strengths and weaknesses in light of the country's prospects for development; they seldom teach their compatriots the lessons that Iran can learn from those countries that have succeeded in the past few decades in significantly improving their people's living conditions. Why is it that Turkey, Malaysia, and South Korea, not to mention China and India, have made tremendous progress toward development over the past three decades, while Iran has, relatively speaking, stagnated? After twenty-eight years of spotty growth, Iran's GNP per capita is barely on a par with the final years of the Shah's government. If growth trends of the last decade of the Shah's government had continued, Iran could have now boasted a standard of living similar to Spain's. Yet that level of achievement seems out of reach in the current international environment. In sharp contrast, numerous countries that started at the same position as Iran—or even lower—back then have managed to double or triple their per capita annual incomes over the past generation. What are the reasons for Iran's underperformance? How can they be remedied?

This chapter discusses the opportunities and challenges facing Iran as it aims to embark on sustainable development. To be sure, development is a multifaceted phenomenon, with interlocking cultural, political, and economic dimensions. Iranians must critically examine those cultural attributes that hinder effective group work and steady progress in their country. They must also search for ways of reforming the country's economic and political structures to be more attuned to the demands of the current time. To be sure, development cannot be achieved by recourse to simplistic and formulaic remedies. It is not sufficient for Iran to merely copy the policies of those countries that have been more successful in instituting developmental policies. While Iran can certainly learn a great deal from such countries, it is important to institute developmental policies that are attuned to Iran's particular attributes, aiming to build on Iran's areas of strength, while redressing the country's shortcomings. Similar to other developing countries, Iran has numerous areas of comparative advantage and disadvantage. Only by acknowledging their national assets and liabilities can Iranians hope to embark on development. Only by fully understanding their current predicament and learning from their past can they hope to build a better future.

Given the currently uncertain position and the credibility problems of multilateral financial institutions—the World Bank and the IMF—that were conceived at Bretton Woods, New Hampshire, after World War II, Iran cannot fully rely on these organizations for direction. In the 1980s and 1990s, especially, the Bretton Woods institutions gave priority to the competitive needs of western multinational companies over and above the welfare of people in whose interests they claimed to be acting. This has often coincided with the undermining of the social fabric of developing countries, and in increasing the divide between rich and poor, both within and between nations. In their dogged determination to promote market solutions to all social ills, these organizations have goaded dozens of countries in the developing world to dismantle their social safety nets and to privatize the basic needs of their people, including water, electricity, transit, and other necessities. These prescriptions, called "structural adjustment," "restructuring," "private sector development," and "shock therapy," have left highly negative effects in their wake from Latin America to Africa and Asia, as hundreds of millions of people have been placed at the mercy of the vagaries of markets that are governed by forces beyond their control.

According to Joseph Stiglitz, who won the Nobel Prize in economics in 2001, and who had served as chief economist at the World Bank and as chairman of the council of economic advisors in the Clinton administration, the forced privatization measures advocated by the World Bank and the IMF worked to exacerbate the problems of poverty that they were supposed to solve. After leaving the World

Bank in 2000, Stiglitz began discussing the need for reforming the "Washington Consensus," which was the term used to describe the neoliberal policies of the Washington-based Bretton Woods institutions. In his books, *Globalization and Its Discontents* and *The Roaring Nineties*, Stiglitz has provided a detailed portrait of the downside of the unprecedented economic boom that was enjoyed by the United States and other developed economies in the 1980s and 1990s. He discussed the ways in which footloose capital undermined the viability and cohesion of dozens of countries in the developing world, whose governments had been rendered powerless by their reliance on the prescriptions of the IMF and the World Bank. Stiglitz proposed a series of fundamental reforms to the structure and policies of these organizations, and charted possible new paths beyond the Washington Consensus.[3] Similar ideas have been advanced by George Soros, the billionaire financier and philanthropist, who has helped popularize the term "International Monetary Fundamentalism" in his various books.[4]

For Iranian policymakers, however, any mention of a Washington Consensus brings to mind another area of agreement, this one within the U.S. government: to contain and weaken Iran by imposing bilateral and multilateral economic sanctions on the country. These policies were enacted in Washington in the mid-1990s, at the same time that the neoliberal vision of the Bretton Woods institutions had, in the wake of the Soviet Union's dissolution, become truly global for the first time. It seems in hindsight that the global vision proposed by U.S. policymakers as well as the leadership of the World Bank and the IMF was more focused on short-term global competitiveness than on long-term global development.

Yet alongside these valid criticisms of the current international economic order, it must also be noted that the 1990s also brought tremendous US-led innovations, especially in the information technology sector, whose benefits have been felt by all countries, including hundreds of millions of people in the developing world. India and China are the most notable examples of countries that have utilized technological advancements to benefit large sections of their populations. The point that critics such as Stiglitz and Soros are making is that the free enterprise system has negative side effects that must be redressed, especially those that headlong privatization leaves in its wake. To be sure, the Bretton Woods institutions have been slow to reform. Any structural change at the World Bank and the IMF will have to coincide with a recognition among the United States and other industrial countries' leadership, that markets dominated by multinational companies are not by themselves capable of bringing welfare and sustainable development to the majority of the world's people. They require judicious state intervention and the input of much stronger nonprofit sectors within the advanced economies and beyond to balance the demands of growth with the need for fair distribution and sustainability, as well as environmental protection.

The simultaneous challenge and opportunity facing Iranian policymakers is that their country is opening up to the world and the main sources of global capital at a time when the stability of the international trading system has been rendered fragile by the excesses of the neoliberal policies of the past three decades. The currently uncertain status of the World Trade Organization, which became the successor to the GATT in 1995, shows how far the world has come in just over a decade in pressing for a correction of the shortcomings of the current international economic order. While joining the WTO remains a stated goal of the Iranian leadership, it is now uncertain what type of organization Iran would be joining if its application for admission were accepted.

The key point here is that change is coming to Iran at the same time that it is coming to the international economic and geopolitical system. If Iranian policymakers can shed their ideological blinders and deal with the new arrangements from the vantage point of knowledge and cooperation—as opposed to reactionary politics—they can be in a position to utilize newly available opportunities to improve the living conditions of Iranians. In so doing, they must remember that while Iran is indeed a significant country in the political and strategic realms, it has an inconsequentially small economy when judged against the global GNP. Given the current exchange rates, Iran's GNP of $200 billion is less than one half of one percent of the global GNP. Thus, expanding their knowledge of the intricacies of the global economy will enable Iranian policymakers to institute developmental policies in their country.

DEVELOPING IRAN'S ENERGY SECTOR

Possessing large deposits of oil and gas has been a mixed blessing for Iran. On the one hand, without its hydrocarbon wealth, it is difficult to imagine where Iran could have found the resources to build its industries and a national infrastructure, especially over the past two generations. At the same time, oil has been a leading cause of Iran's international disputes and the source of uneven development in the country. Reliance on the export of crude oil has entrenched a rent-seeking culture among Iranians, who have come to rely on the government to bring them welfare and development, and in Khomeini's oft-quoted promise before the revolution, to "bring free oil to their doorsteps." Since the oil industry is owned by the government, and since the industry is not labor intensive, the government has not been able to redress the lingering problem of unemployment across the country by relying on the energy sector. On the contrary, revenue from oil exports has traditionally acted as a disincentive for Iranians to invest in other productive enterprises; it has also hampered the development of a competitive private sector in Iran, whose revenues the government could tax and invest in the country's productive potential. Thus, being entrapped by the "rentier-state" mentality has set Iran's economic and political development back considerably.

Another major problem posed by reliance on oil is the volatility of its price. In 1998, for example, the price of oil dipped to $12 per barrel. In the run-up to the U.S.-led invasion of Iraq in 2003, the price of oil was in the 25-dollar range. Beginning in 2003, as the folly of the war became evident, the price of oil shot up and reached $70 in 2006. At the time of this writing, oil trades at $60 per barrel. Such extreme volatility implies that economic planning in Iran and other oil-dependent countries is completely beholden to the vagaries of oil price fluctuations. Perversely, it has been international instability, led by conflict in the Persian Gulf region, which has led to a precipitous rise in the price of oil. Thus, from an oil-dependent Iranian perspective, instability in Iran's region has noticeably raised Iran's earnings. From this shortsighted vantage point, the Iranian government would seem to have an interest in maintaining its adversarial stance toward the United States in the Persian Gulf region and beyond. Yet this can hardly be seen as a long-term and sustainable solution to the country's need for pro-development economic planning. In this particular sense, oil has been an especially harmful factor in Iran's quest for sustainable economic growth, and for the competitiveness of the country's industries.

To be sure, all countries that are dependent on raw resources as their main earners of hard currency are similarly affected by the "resource curse." Yet countries with smaller populations than Iran—such as the Arab monarchies of the Persian Gulf region, or even Venezuela—can afford to rely on oil far into the future far more than Iran can. This is the case also because these countries do not have the high level of domestic energy consumption that Iran has. While all oil-dependent economies are vulnerable to the fluctuations in the price of oil, this problem is especially acute for Iran. Another major difference between Iran and other leading oil exporters is that Iran is locked in seemingly endless disputes with the world's main industrial powers, especially the United States, and thus it has not been able to raise its production capacity to a level commensurate with the country's vast reserves and large population. As noted above, after Saudi Arabia, Iran holds the second highest level of oil reserves in the world. Given sufficient care and investment, the country has the potential to significantly expand its exports in the upstream and downstream sectors. But since the energy sector, more so than most other businesses, is deeply entangled with international politics, Iran's adversarial relationship with the United States and other major powers has led to the emergence of a consensus that Iran's oil and gas sectors should be prevented from progressing to their potential, lest this enable Iranian leaders to become more ambitious in their designs for the region that surrounds Iran and beyond. In short, to optimally benefit from its oil and gas riches, Iran must work to remove the main sources of its disputes with countries that have the capacity to help raise the performance of Iran's energy sector to international standards. Similar to its nuclear program, Iran's oil and gas sector will continue to be significantly beset by the distrust of major powers in the Iranian leadership's intentions. The uniquely strident declarations of Iranian leaders, especially President Ahmadinejad, have given enough ammunition to Iran's adversaries to prove the source of their concern.

The extraction and export of crude oil was the leading source of hard currency for Iran over most of the twentieth century. Today, oil remains the source of over 80 percent of the country's hard currency earnings, and serves as the backbone of the country's solvency. It is indeed difficult to imagine what life in Iran would be like in the absence of oil revenues. Despite the centrality of the country's energy sector, however, Iran has not succeeded in attracting large-scale investment to refurbish its aging oil fields and to expand its declining refining capacity. Equally significant is the underdeveloped Iranian natural gas industry that, if developed fully, can supply the whole world with natural gas for thirty years.

The total amount of foreign investment Iran has attracted to its energy sector since the revolution is in the single-digit billions of dollars, even though it has had the capacity for absorbing over ten times as much. This is one reason Iran's oil production and exports have significantly lagged their potential. In the mid-1970s, Iran reached an all-time high in oil production as it pumped 6 million barrels per day, exporting over 5 million bpd. At that time, along with Saudi Arabia, Iran was OPEC's leading oil exporter. Thirty years later, Iran's oil production is barely above 4 million bpd. As the country's population has doubled in this period, the oil left for export has dwindled to 2.6 million bpd, which is about half the oil Iran exported in the final years of the Shah's government. Despite record high oil prices in 2005–2007, which have averaged over $60 per barrel, earning Iran over $50 billion per year in this period, Iran has not been able to significantly raise its production and refining capacity. If Iran is unable to raise its capacity with record oil prices, its prospects in this area will be decidedly less sanguine with lower oil prices.

Nowhere is Iran's underachievement in the energy sector on more vivid display than in the country's inability to produce enough refined gasoline to fuel its vehicles. Currently, Iran imports $5 billion worth of gasoline a year, about half its consumption, to meet growing domestic demand. The government then subsidizes gasoline prices by selling it at the pumps at 10 cents a liter, at a small fraction of what it costs to import. This incentive to drive is a leading cause of urban air pollution and crippling traffic, especially in the capital, Tehran. Numerous economic experts, within and outside the government, have advised Iranian leaders to reduce and then end the country's reliance on imported gasoline. While acknowledging the importance of this problem, however, the government has delayed serious attempts at dealing with it. One of the main, though little discussed, reasons for this policy is the fact that a significant portion of middle-class Iranians in the largest cities, unable to support themselves through their regular jobs, work as amateur taxi drivers in their private vehicles. Moonlighting is thus the most common occupation in Iranian cities, especially in Tehran. Subsidized gasoline is the government's perverse way of creating jobs for an otherwise wayward and idle population, whose broad-based unemployment could lead to widespread unrest if gasoline prices rose noticeably.

Thus, double-digit unemployment and widespread underemployment, and the concomitant fear of social upheaval, are the main reasons for the country's artificially low gasoline prices, and the main source of the need for continuing gasoline imports. The overflow of cars on Tehran and other cities' roads, and poor urban planning, are the main causes of the low quality of life for urban dwellers. It is customary for Tehran residents to complain that crossing the city can take as much as three to four hours. Tehran's crippling traffic has a devastating effect on Iranian workers' efficiency, as much of their productive energy is sapped in getting to work and back. In addition, rising domestic consumption of subsidized oil products cuts into the country's capacity for exports, and thus reduces Iran's hard currency earnings in this area.

A successful attempt at increasing Iran's oil and gas production would have to be based on attracting up to $10 billion a year of foreign investment to the country's energy sector. This goal, as noted above, can only be reached if Iran addresses the main sources of its tense relationship with the international community, especially so in the case of the United States and European countries. While Iran could benefit from the technical know-how of American, Japanese, Italian, French, British, Russian, and Chinese companies, it can also attract capital from the GCC countries, which have posted record earnings in the past few years, and which have embarked on an ambitious drive to invest on all continents. Thus, even more so than other parts of its economy, Iran's strategic energy sector is dependent on reliable and peaceful international partnerships.

One of the most astute observers of Iran's energy sector is Narsi Ghorban, who completed his doctoral studies in energy economics in Britain in the late 1970s. After the revolution, he has worked as a researcher and commentator in Iran. In a series of essays that were published by the *Middle East Economic Survey* throughout the 1990s and after, Ghorban has argued for the need to restructure Iran's energy sector to make it more competitive and profitable. In September 1997, writing in *MEES* following the election of the reformist Mohammad Khatami as Iran's president, Ghorban made astute recommendations to the incoming administration.[5] He suggested that Iran should separate the oil ministry from the state-run oil and gas companies to reduce political interference in the sector's activities; create an effective national gas company and a corresponding gas law; find suitable mechanisms for attracting domestic and foreign sources of expertise and capital to the oil and gas sector; adopt more transparent accounting practices; and create the conditions for greater private sector involvement in the country's energy sector. Eight years after these recommendations, Ghorban wrote again in *MEES*, appraising the progress that had been made in these areas during this period.[6] On the whole, while acknowledging progress in implementing the spirit of the above and similar recommendations, Ghorban argued that the same problems still stymied progress, despite the Khatami government's acknowledgment of the need for change.

On the issue of separating the Oil Ministry from the business activities of the three main Iranian energy companies—National Iranian Oil Company (NIOC), National Iranian Gas Company (NIGC), and National Petrochemical Company (NPC)—it is evident that little has changed over the past decade. Not only does the Oil Ministry serve a macro-level policy function, it also meddles in the operational and business activities of the three main Iranian energy companies. This is especially the case since the heads of the above companies are chosen by the oil minister, and serve as deputy ministers. The overt political interference in choosing these deputy ministers has meant that people with insufficient technical knowledge of the energy sector are often given leadership positions. Bridging the knowledge gap between political appointees and technical managers has been one of the most important shortcomings of industrial management in Iran since the revolution. Of particular relevance is the fact that government bureaucrats often act beyond their legislated roles as macro-level policymakers and micromanage all aspects of production and marketing, making the process inefficient and overly politicized.

Given the annual decline rate of over 200,000 bpd (barrels per day) in Iran's crude oil production capacity, there is a need for large-scale investments for developing new fields and for massive gas injection to maintain Iran's share of OPEC and world production. It is estimated that about $40 billion of investment is needed in the upstream crude oil sector to create an extra capacity of 2–2.5mn bpd in five years. According to Bjian Namdar-Zangeneh, Iran's oil minister in the Khatami government, Iran has the capacity to absorb $150 billion in its oil, gas, and petrochemical industries over a decade. In such a scenario, the country could pump as much oil as Saudi Arabia, which would imply returning to the parity that existed between the two OPEC leaders at the time of the Shah.[7]

In 1997, Ghorban had proposed that the NIGC be built as an integrated gas company, similar to Russia's Gazprom, British Gas, and Gaz de France. He had suggested that the new company operate independently from daily government interference to be able to cooperate and compete with major international companies in the gas sector. The new and improved NIGC would be responsible for handling the exploration, development, and marketing of Iranian gas, with the authority to enter agreements with domestic and international partners. Yet Iran still lacks a comprehensive gas strategy. With 940 trillion cubic feet of gas reserves, Iran is ideally positioned to meet the gas demands of the growing economies in Asia and Europe, and to generate billions of dollars of annual profit from these exports. But the country's export of gas is negligible given its potential. While Iran has about half as much gas as Russia, its exports are about 2 percent of Russia's exports. Since gas is a clean-burning fuel, developing its resources in this sector is vital for Iran. To be able to optimally harness this resource, however, Iran needs the cooperation of partners on all continents. It also needs a professional cadre of managers and technical experts to develop its gas resources and to market it to consumers worldwide. Political obstacles within Iran and friction with international sources of capital and know-how have significantly set back Iran's prospects in this area.

Another key issue in the development of Iran's energy sector is the suboptimal knowledge base within the country. This requires the establishment of new centers within Iranian universities and research facilities to research and teach the technical and international aspects of the energy business. These centers would ideally maintain close contacts with countries that are more advanced than Iran in the energy sector. A crucial area for further development in Iran is the discipline of energy economics and the geoeconomics of energy. Given the excessive politicization of the oil and gas sector in Iran, the country also faces a shortage of skilful negotiators, who would be knowledgeable about the country's particular energy assets and about the international energy markets. Since the oil minister and his deputies are the final negotiators of Iran's oil and gas contracts, the Iranian energy sector, with a few exceptions, does not have qualified legal and economic experts to optimally advance Iran's interests.

As Ghorban has argued in his essays in *MEES*, this inattention to technical expertise has led to a situation where engineers are put in charge of international negotiations while economists and legal experts meddle in the technical aspects of oil and gas production. It is necessary for Iranian policymakers to recognize the need for respecting specialization and the necessity of allowing appropriately trained experts to handle the different aspects of developing the country's oil and gas reserves and bringing them to the market.

While Iran has enough oil and gas to power its economy for another fifty years, it is crucial to realize that the world's advanced economies have been awakened to the dangers of global warming, which has been wrought by excessive reliance on fossil fuels. As the world invests in nuclear, solar, and other cleaner sources of energy, its reliance on fossil fuels will lessen. The design of hybrid cars is likely to increasingly move the world's main economies away from imported oil. In other words, Iran has a chance to maximally benefit from oil and gas exports in the next two or three decades, but not much beyond. This reality should compel Iranian leaders to maximally harness their oil and gas reserves in an expedient manner and to take fundamental steps to diversify their economy and reduce its dependence on energy exports.

A declared policy of Khatami's government was advancing privatization across the country's industries, including the energy sector. All ministers, including the oil minister, publicly supported this policy, which was based on article 44 of the Iranian constitution, which makes provisions for the active involvement of the private sector in running the country's economy. Despite its initial resistance, the Ahmadinejad government has similarly paid lip service to the need for privatization, including that of the lucrative oil and gas sector. Yet the progress of the drive toward private-sector involvement has been slow, especially since the Iranian private sector lacks the resources to become a significant partner in the energy sector. The key challenge for the government is to empower the private sector with loans and access to the industry's infrastructure. Since oil and gas are viewed as national commodities, it is essential for the government to utilize the private sector's involvement in advancing economic development in other sectors. In other words, since oil and gas play such a central role in the economy, the challenge of effective policymaking is to ensure that the wealth generated by domestic and foreign investors trickles down to the population as a whole. Given the negative record of privatization as conceived by the Washington Consensus in the past two to three decades, it is necessary to conceive a different form of privatization where the profit incentive and entrepreneurship of private actors can be harnessed to benefit the country as a whole, not for it to become the exclusive purview of a well-connected minority. This is a challenge that Iran and other developing countries face not only in their most important sectors, but across their economies.

To deal with this particular challenge, Iran can look to Malaysia and South Korea as models. In both of these cases, the state has been the main enabler of the private sector's growth, while requiring private owners of industries to pay their taxes in full and to invest in the national infrastructure, guided by a long-term vision. However, the main difference between Iran and such highly successful countries is that, unlike Iran, they have not been burdened by ideological friction with the main sources of international capital. In addition, such countries' populations have more disciplined work ethics than Iranians. Their political and economic cultures are more amenable to development than Iran's. In its drive toward development, Iran must compare and contrast its national attributes with these countries and search for ways it can learn from their successful record of developing their economies over the past three decades.

One of the most important achievements of the previous administrations in Iran has been the enactment of the Oil Stabilization Fund (OSF) in the year 2000.[8] According to Jehangir Amuzegar, a prominent Iranian-American economist, the OSF was created to act as a cushion against the instability caused by widely fluctuating price of oil; to maintain fiscal and budget discipline to regulate public spending; enabling steady economic planning; and to maintain the stability of the oil-backed Iranian currency, the riyal. While these goals are universally viewed as laudable, there have been serious problems associated with Iran's OSF. If the fund is not well integrated into the national budget, it will create a parallel machinery for budgeting and will negatively affect sound fiscal and monetary policy. Second, the OSF is likely to reduce transparency of the government's budgeting process.

The necessity of creating a buffer to guard against the vagaries of oil prices had been made obvious to Iranian economic policymakers in 1986, and then in 1997–1998, when oil prices dipped to record lows, throwing the country's budgeting mechanism into disarray. The OSF has thus been viewed as a mechanism for guarding against the "resource curse." The Third Five-Year Development Plan of Islamic Republic, which covered the 2000–2005 period, mandated the country's Central Bank to create an "oil foreign exchange reserve account" to stabilize the budgeting needs of the country. According to the plan, once the budget's commitments are met, the government should deposit surplus revenues from the export of oil in the fund. Conversely, in years when the government's revenues are insufficient for covering budgetary outlays, the government can dip into the fund to cover its shortcomings. An amendment was added to the plan's original prescriptions in November 2000, instructing the government to set aside 50 percent of the fund's revenues to provide low-interest loans to local entrepreneurs engaged in productive and employment-creating enterprises.

According to Amuzegar, despite its laudable intentions, Iran's OSF suffers from serious shortcomings. First is the fact that, unlike successful funds in other oil-exporting countries, such as the Norwegian Petroleum Fund, Iran's OSF does not seek to invest its resources in profitable enterprises abroad. Indeed, one of the hallmarks of the world's successful economies is their ability to invest in profitable enterprises internationally. Iran's record has been especially deficient in this area. Another key deficiency, as noted above, is the lack of a transparent reporting mechanism that can provide an accurate sense for the fund's reserves and performance.

According to the Third Plan's projections, based on the oil price of $12–19 per barrel, Iran was slated to earn $57 billion from the export of oil in 2000–2005. Yet the unexpected rise in the price of oil meant that Iran earned over twice the projected figure. According to the Plan's directives, the government was supposed to deposit about $70 billion in the OSF. Yet the government's total deposits into the OSF amounted to $30 billion. The Iranian parliament, the Majles, and the government ignored the Plan's directives and dipped into the OSF for $17 billion to finance a variety of subsidies and government-run development projects, including new payments to government-run volunteer militia, the Basij, and to the veterans of the Iran-Iraq war, who are viewed as the main constituencies of the current government. This inattention to the prescriptions of the Third Plan meant that the OSF's original purpose has been all but ignored during Ahmadinejad's presidency. The main purpose of the OSF's establishment had been adopting a long-term vision of Iran's economic well-being. More focused on currying short-term favors from their constituents, the current government has embarked on a perilous course of discounting the future. While working-class Iranians have seen the benefits of the government's largesse over the short term, they are not likely to benefit from these policies in the long term. While Ahmadinejad came to power on a platform of fighting poverty, his government's policies are not likely to address the roots of Iran's underdevelopment. Instead, he and his allies in the Majles have chosen the path of short-term political expediency, made possible by record oil prices, to stave off public discontent, and to pave the way for his reelection in 2009.

In the meantime, Ahmadinejad has dismantled the independent Plan and Budget Organization, which was supposed to oversee the OSF. He has incorporated the organization into the presidential office and turned it into a tactical tool of the government. Early in his presidency, Ahmadinejad also chose a similar course in his choice of oil minister. In nominating individuals who had little experience in the industry but who were his close political allies, Ahmadinejad showed that he wished to bring the energy sector under the presidential office's direct control. Yet the Majles rejected his first three nominees and settled on a compromise candidate with more experience in the oil ministry, Kazem Hamaneh Vaziri, who was better known among the country's oil industry managers. Ahmadinejad's first nominee, Ali Saeedlou, who had little experience in the energy sector, currently serves as Iran's executive vice president.

THE CHALLENGE OF ECONOMIC REFORM

Beginning in the second term of Khatami's presidency, in early 2002, the Iranian government began a series of market-oriented economic reforms. These included unifying the exchange rate, which had eluded the government since the early 1980s; ratifying the law on protecting foreign investment; tax reforms; and making provisions for the establishment of three private banks.[9]

These initiatives indicated that Iranian policymakers had become aware that their economic policymaking had to be reformed to increase the country's prospects for development. In the preceding two decades, since the revolution, the Iranian economy had experienced a significant decline. While in the period 1960–1975 the GDP per capita had doubled, by 1990 this figure had declined to about half the figure in 1975. To make matters worse, Iran has had to contend with high inflation and unemployment rates, both of which seem to be resistant to the windfalls that accrue to Iran when oil prices rise, especially since, as we discussed above, oil windfalls have not been invested in enhancing the country's productive potential, and have been used for short-term political expediency and for other "band-aid solutions." The decline in Iran's economic performance has also been exacerbated by external factors, the most important of which have been the eight-year war with Iraq, which destroyed much of Iran's industrial infrastructure; primary and secondary economic sanctions by the United States and the freezing of Iran's assets; capital flight and brain drain, and widely fluctuating oil prices. Seen together, the instability of the domestic and international environment for Iran has worked to undermine the country's prospects for development.

According to Parvin Alizadeh, a "structural trap" is largely responsible for Iran's economic doldrums. The term refers to a situation in which political and structural obstacles prevent the allocation of resources from low productivity and unprofitable firms to high productivity and profitable ones. According to Alizadeh, the presence of unaccountable revolutionary organizations and foundations, which control large parts of the economy, have been major contributors to this malaise. For close to two decades after the revolution of 1979, the role of the private sector in the Iranian economy witnessed a precipitous decline. The large-scale nationalization of the 1980s meant that the government cared more about short-term redistributive policies than about long-term national productivity. After the revolution, with the flight of the industrialist class, the government embarked on a massive confiscation of property and handing it to the "dispossessed" classes. This policy was also followed in the changing ownership of Iran's large industrial enterprises in the steel, auto, and other heavy industry sectors, which were most dependent on managerial know-how. The placing of such assets in the hands of untrained, government-picked managers meant that Iran's industrial and manufacturing sector, which had been painstakingly built over decades by the Shah's government, lost its competitive edge.[10]

It is important to note that state-owned enterprises can be harbingers of economic development. But to do so, as has been the case in South Korea and Taiwan, the state must impose discipline on these industries and focus their activities on the promotion of exports. By closely monitoring their performance, the state in these countries has compelled them to raise their standards to globally competitive levels. It is true that South Korean and Taiwanese state-owned enterprises benefited from government subsidies in their formative years, but these subsidies were allocated for fixed periods. In Iran's case, by contrast, state subsidies have functioned as open-ended sources of support, and they have robbed these enterprises—especially the heavy industries—of any incentive to become competitive and profitable. This policy has also fed corruption, as the means of production have been placed in the hands of the cronies of the country's political leaders. In this sense, Iran's performance of encouraging inefficient state-led enterprise more closely resembles that of the former Soviet Union and other Eastern Block countries.

Shielded from international competition by oil-based subsidies, Iran's state-owned enterprises have been a main cause of Iran's economic doldrums since the revolution. Specifically, state-owned enterprises in Iran have undermined the country's economy in three ways. First, they have exerted powerful inflationary pressures on the economy. One of the main reasons for Iran's reckless monetary policies in the postrevolutionary period, which have led to excessive liquidity, is the generous subsidies that the government has offered to money-losing enterprises. In the words of Hashem Pesaran, a leading economist at Cambridge University, "In the final analysis the main cause of excessive monetary expansion and inflation have to be found in the government's unwillingness to oppose the credit demand of politically powerful groups (both inside and outside the government)."[11]

The second negative impact of state-owned firms on the Iranian economy has been their inability to create sufficient jobs for the burgeoning labor force. The private sector remains the main provider of employment to Iranians, with over 70 percent of the country's jobs. Despite the massive capital outlays that have been sunk into state-owned enterprises, only about a quarter of employment opportunities in Iran are provided by the government or state-owned enterprises. The third major problem posed by state-owned enterprises has been their lack of transparency. Since they lack shareholders, in the traditional sense of the term, these organizations are accountable to no one other than their political patrons. Nor does the Iranian parliament have the authority to demand that they provide accurate facts and figures from their activities. Given the foregoing discussion on the negative impact of open-ended subsidies on Iran's development prospects, it is essential to see noncompetitive state-owned industries as key components of the system of patronage in Iran, which hinders the expansion of the country's productive potential.

Attentive to these issues, Iran's supreme leader, Seyed Ali Khamenei, in early 2007, chided the economic performance of Ahmadinejad's government by re-declaring his support for article 44 of the Iranian constitution, which is based on allowing private ownership of the means of production. Yet, bedeviled by the resource curse, with the currently high oil prices, the government is unlikely to enter uncharted waters, which might raise the risk of public unrest. A much safer course of action in the short term is to maintain the status quo and to appease well-connected constituents. Yet leaving these tough decisions to future administrations cannot be viewed as responsible and pro-development policymaking. It can be argued that it was low oil prices during the Khatami years that led to the positive policymaking on the economic front. The challenge of progressive policymaking is to make tough decisions, even if they are not pressing in the short term. Most pressing in this area is respecting the mandate of the Oil Stabilization Fund, and to utilize its reserves for improving the country's long-term productive capacity, not, as is now the case, as an exclusive dispenser of short-term relief.

THE PLIGHT OF THE POOR AND RURAL DEVELOPMENT

While the ideologically based economic policy of the Iranian government since the revolution has generally failed at improving the country's economic performance, the government's performance in aiding the poor and the disadvantaged rural areas has been positive. The most comprehensive research on the improvements in these areas and the remaining challenges has been produced by the Iranian-American economist, Djavad Salehi-Isfahani.[12]

Salehi-Isfahani has outlined the demographic trends that bode well for the country's development. Because of effective government intervention, fertility rates in Iran are at a manageable rate, around 1.3 percent per year. Rural educational programs and birth control education have expanded beyond the cities and reached the countryside. Similarly, literacy rates in the countryside have expanded considerably in the past two decades, and reached 80 percent. This is a significant improvement over the 30 percent rate of literacy in the rural areas prior to the revolution. The most effective and far-reaching program of the government after the Iran-Iraq war was the rural health and family programs that began under Rafsanjani's two-term presidency (1989–1997). At the time, the success of these programs was acknowledged by international organizations such as the World Bank and the UN.[13]

The evidence provided by Salehi-Isfahani shows that extreme poverty has substantially declined in recent years, especially in the years preceding Ahmadinejad's election to the presidency in 2005. This has been especially the case in the increased access of the poor to basic necessities such as electricity, drinking water, and to household appliances and public health provisions.

This shows that more than increasing poverty rates, it is increased expectations and grievances based on perceived injustice that drive populist sentiments in Iran. To get an accurate sense of the ways in which poverty has been reduced in Iran after the revolution, it is necessary to examine per capita incomes and expenditures. Such data show that, on average, economic well-being has been advancing among the poor. While Salehi-Isfahani's claim that Iran's GDP per capita has been restored to the prerevolutionary levels cannot be substantiated with exchange rate data— one U.S. dollar was worth 70 riyals before the revolution; today it is worth 9,000 riyals—his evidence-based argument that the poor have noticeably improved their lot since the revolution is correct.

Despite these positive developments, however, a key problem facing the Iranian economy is high unemployment among the country's young population. Among those who are twenty to twenty-four years old, unemployment is at close to 40 percent. This forces middle-class and low-income families into shouldering the burden of supporting their children well into the latter's late twenties and even thirties. Another significant problem is the fact that employment and advancement prospects for the country's youth remain far less promising than they were for the generation that entered the job market thirty years ago. A key source of discontent is the lack of job security. While stringent labor legislation that makes the termination of employment contracts difficult is a main feature of Iran's labor laws, private sector employers have resorted to short-term contracts, especially when hiring unskilled laborers. These workers have also been stung by competitive pressures from Asian suppliers whose access to cheap labor has made it uneconomical for Iranian industries to remain productive, especially in the textile, leather goods, and machine tools industries.

According to Salehi-Isfahani, the majority of Iranians who express dissatisfaction with their economic plight have an exaggerated sense of the extent of the country's oil income, especially for a country of 70 million people. Thus, they feel that government policy has failed them by not providing them with their just share of the national wealth. Given the government's rhetorical commitment to social justice, raised expectations lead to increased feelings of discontent. Beginning in the prerevolutionary period, excessive reliance on oil revenues meant that Iranians developed a "rentier" mentality based on the assumption that they deserve welfare and progress without having to acquire competitive work skills. Iranians should realize that even with record oil sales—which topped $50 billion in 2006—for a population of 70 million, the per capita oil income is less than $500 a year once subsidies are paid. Even for low-income Iranians, this figure can barely cover subsistence needs at a very basic level. This means that only by investing in the country's productive capacity and a long-term vision can the government deliver on its promise of instituting sustainable economic development.

EDUCATION FOR DEVELOPMENT

While ribbon-cutting ceremonies at mega projects such as hydroelectric dams are popular among Iranian leaders, the key resource Iran possesses is its human capital. With steadily rising literacy rates in the country, especially in rural areas, the postrevolutionary government has made positive strides in bringing previously marginalized strata into the national fold. Yet despite this achievement, the idea of "education for development" has still not taken root in the country. With the expansion of the state-run and private universities in the country, increasing numbers have been exposed to higher education. Today, half the country's university seats are occupied by women. This, too, is a major achievement. What has been missing so far is a matching of the country's development needs with the teaching of appropriate skills to broad sections of the population.

Currently Iran has two dozen universities that offer master's and doctoral programs in the physical and social sciences. Afflicted by what is called the "diploma disease" in the economic development literature, however, talented Iranians have sought to receive graduate education in fields for which there are few employment opportunities. An increasing number of the country's best and brightest have therefore been educated at the public treasury's expense, only to emigrate to industrialized countries where their skills can be put to use. While the number of degree-granting universities has mushroomed, the country still lags in providing technical education. For Iran today, far more pressing than the granting of master's and doctoral degrees is the development of capable technicians and business managers. Such a redirected focus can begin to remedy the country's unemployment crisis. It can also focus Iranians' attention on the specific needs of their country as they seek to improve their employment and advancement prospects.

As we noted above, development is a multifaceted phenomenon, with economic, political, and cultural components. The cultural aspects of development refer to those habits of behavior and thinking that a people must attain to be able to embark on stable progress. Unfortunately, the Iranian educational system has been highly deficient at the secondary and postsecondary levels in teaching people about what these habits are. While such cultural underpinnings of development are rarely discussed in the economic development literature inside Iran and abroad, for a country such as Iran, they are perhaps the most important prerequisites of development.

One of the most significant obstacles to progress in Iran is the fact that the people see development as something that is supposed to be handed out overnight by the government. The role of the people themselves is far less frequently discussed. At the same time, Iranians are highly individualistic and group work in the country remains undisciplined and laden with exorbitant transaction costs. For visitors to Iran from the industrialized countries, it seems as though a general chaos prevails across the country. Nowhere is this more evident than in the inattention of most Iranians to the rules of driving and orderly social behavior. How can a country develop successfully, after all, when over 20,000 people die every year on its roads in traffic accidents? Iranian roads have the distinction of being the most dangerous in the world. How can business proceed with efficiency when Tehran's traffic, among the worst in the world, makes it virtually impossible to get to one's destination on time? The prevailing chaos in Iran is such a steady feature of social life that the Persian language has dedicated a specific saying to describe it. Compared to industrialized countries, life in Iran is considered to be "shir-to-shir" which means "lion-in-lion."

Addressing the overwhelming chaos of Iranian social life is the most crucial aspect of development planning in Iran. The government can impose stiffer penalties on traffic and other infractions that undermine social order. Yet given the fact that bribery of the underpaid traffic police and other law enforcement officers is common in Iran, it is unlikely that punishments alone can achieve this objective. Far more effective would be a national educational program that engages all Iranians in a discussion of how their country is set back by the chaos that prevails in their social life. A simple but effective method might be to show films of how traffic moves in other large cities and to contrast that with the kamikaze driving habits of Iranians. Since Iranians are a proud people with a rich national heritage, they might be asked, "Why can't we behave and drive in the same orderly fashion that people in developed countries do?" "Why can't we respect the rules of orderly social behavior?" Such training should become a pillar of K–12 education in Iran.

As noted above, the Iranian educational system on all levels must be redesigned to reflect the specific needs of the country. Publicly funded education, in particular, must benefit from an input-output analysis that gives priority to the country's specific needs. While Iranians enjoy being called "Dr." and "engineer," they must be taught that the country needs skilled professionals in all fields. Becoming certified and reliable electricians, truck drivers, mechanics, machine tools makers and other skilled industrial workers should be accorded the same prestige as doctors and engineers. This is especially pressing now that a sizeable portion of Iran's doctors, engineers, and PhDs find it highly difficult to find gainful employment in their fields, and resort to a variety of jobs that are beneath their skill levels. This causes tremendous strain and dejection among the country's professional classes.

Another key feature of a program of education for development is the realization that advancement comes with skill, dedication, and hard work. Since the revolution, especially, with the flight of the managerial and industrialist class from Iran, the new rich have emanated from the country's merchant class in the Bazaar. The amassing of astronomical fortunes in a short period has been based on hoarding, speculation, and other unproductive pursuits. Educated Iranians look in dejection and anger at "crony capitalists" who have grown rich virtually overnight, without creating jobs, investing in the country's infrastructure, or enhancing its competitiveness. Since the government is the ultimate source of capital and credit in Iran, the population's grievance is often directed at the government for being the ultimate patron of such merchants.

During the Pahlavi era, Iran developed a highly skilled managerial class that was attuned to the culture of industry and competitiveness. After the revolution, however, since the government saw such managers and industrialists as western influences, the whole idea of rank and professionalism was undermined significantly. Since in the eyes of Islam all people are equal, hence, the whole idea of management and division of labor was eschewed. To be sure, beginning in the Rafsanjani and Khatami administrations, steps were taken to remedy this situation, but given the clerics' meddling in all aspects of national policymaking—including industrial planning, for which they are indisputably unqualified—the country's chains of command and the general efficiency of national life have been significantly undermined. Knowledge of the Koran and other heavenly issues has little utility when dealing with matters of technical competence.

The above discussion on the need for depoliticizing the country's energy sector applies to all sectors of the economy. Iran needs a system in which meritocracy is at the core of national policymaking. Nowhere is this more important than in development planning and in the need for instituting effective management practices. Being a devout follower of Iranian leadership, by itself, is insufficient for leading and managing the country's budding industrial enterprises. Nowhere is this more pressing than in sectors with high growth and export potential, especially so in the case of Iran's petrochemical industry.

Development planning in Iran has a relatively long history. Iran's Planning Organization was created in 1949. From that time until the revolution of 1979, five comprehensive plans were drafted and implemented in Iran. Despite significant progress in Iran during this time, however, the country's development was uneven and erratic. This was due partially to the Shah and his underlings' exclusive control over all aspects of economic policymaking, and partially to the vagaries of fluctuating oil prices that undermined the attempts at planning. Similarly, the attempt at instituting steady progress in Iran after the revolution, while successful in some areas, has been undermined by a series of internal and external factors.

Iranians have come a long way in the past fifty years. Their knowledge base in the sciences and technology has expanded and reached the far corners of the country. What is needed in setting the country on a steady course toward development is a national dialogue and practices that overcome reactionary and ideological approaches to policymaking. Every time Iran's current leadership justify their policies by referring to God and the prophets, they delay the pressing need for an honest, objective, and thoroughgoing discussion of what the role of government, private industry, and the people should be if the country is to reach its potential. The recent record prices of oil have only further delayed the heeding of this acute need.

Iranians and their leaders must take responsibility for their current plight. Blaming other countries for Iran's condition, while politically expedient in the short term, is harmful to the country's development prospects as it feeds the Iranian tendency to blame their plight on forces beyond their control. Iranians need to become, in thought, discourse, and deed, masters of their own fate. Only then can Iran become a place of hope and steady progress well into the future.

Part III

Prospects for the Future

CHAPTER FIVE

The Culture of Development

As the thirtieth anniversary of the 1979 revolution approaches, Iranians glance at their country's future with a mixture of hope and trepidation: hope because they have learned a great deal about their own strengths and weaknesses in the postrevolutionary period, and trepidation because a government that calls itself "Islamic" and rules in the name of God seems unfit for the demands of life in the early twenty-first century. How can Islamic tenets created fourteen centuries ago be used to regulate life in the modern world? This is an especially poignant question for Iran that, by Asian standards, has an established history of democratic institutions, which began with the constitutional revolution of 1906.

Today's Iran remains the world's sole theocracy. Of the 192 member countries of the UN, 57 of which are in the Muslim world, it is only in Iran that the clergy wield supreme political power, and claim their unilateral right to rule, not from the consent of the governed, nor from any modern precedents, but from the "will of God." Since God's will isn't readily recognizable to fallible humans, nor laid out in specific detail in any human document of contemporary relevance, it falls on the clergy to interpret divine demands and the laws of Islam as they see fit. Such instrumental and politicized interpretation of Islam has proved to be harmful to politics and religion alike; it has devalued both Iran and Islam. It is undeniable that the clergy, led by Khomeini, played the lead role in the revolution's victory. Islam in general, and the Shia faith in particular, constitute important sources of the culture and identity of Iranians. The concerns presented herein about the appropriateness of religious rule in today's Iran are not intended to downgrade the value of Islam as a religion. Rather, these critiques are presented to preserve the positive aspects of Islam in the national life of Iranians.

This chapter examines issues of democracy and popular sovereignty in Iran in the postrevolutionary period. It discusses the relationship between Islam and the state in Iran after the revolution by drawing on the insights of leading religious reformists such as Abdolkarim Soroush, Seyed Mohammad Khatami, and

Akbar Ganji. The importance of their contribution is that they have provided a critique of religious rule utilizing its own terms. Then, we discuss diversity and multiculturalism in the country, and the issue of women's rights in Iran. To be sure, modifying the current political system in Iran has to occur with the cooperation of Iran's religious leaders, especially the country's supreme leader, Seyed Ali Khamenei, who has led Iran since 1989. In our opinion, to be productive and lasting, change must come to Iran gradually, peacefully, and from within. As the revolution of 1979 showed, mass uprisings produce unintended consequences that are often beyond the control of social and political leaders. In discussing the necessity of separating religion from day-to-day politics, we acknowledge the necessity of preserving the Iranian people's faith in Islam, and ensuring that political expediency doesn't tarnish the image of one of the world's great religions in the eyes of Iranians. Similarly, we hope to show that infringements of human rights by the ruling clerical establishment in Iran cannot be blamed on Islam, but on a politicized and instrumental view of religion that has altered the tenets of the faith to suit its immediate political needs.

Before returning to Iran in 1979 after fourteen years of exile, Khomeini had declared that he was not interested in exercising political power, and that he saw his role as a unifier of diverse strata who opposed the monarchical regime. He had said that upon the revolution's victory, he would retire to his religious teaching in the holy city of Qum. Yet upon returning to Iran, Khomeini did not honor his promise, and in fact did the exact opposite. He settled in Tehran and began directing all aspects of policymaking. He also presided over the executions of tens of thousands of Iranians who, in his opinion, did not conform sufficiently to his Islamic government's demands.

THE LEGACY OF RELIGIOUS REFORM

The election of the reformist cleric Seyed Mohammad Khatami to the presidency of Iran on May 23, 1997, was a watershed in postrevolutionary Iranian history. Over twenty million Iranians voted for Khatami, electing him with a two-thirds majority. The huge popular mandate garnered by Khatami's campaign was largely attributable to the fact that Khatami and his reformist ideas were not endorsed by the conservative clerical establishment. Khatami himself had not been well known among Iranians, and had served as minister of culture for four years in the government of his predecessor, Akbar Hashemi Rafsanjani, and as head of the national library since then.

Khatami's gathering popularity during his two-month campaign owed much to his open and tolerant interpretation of Islam, and his emphasis on the compatibility of reason and religion. The majority of Iranians, it seemed, keen to maintain their attachment to the positive features of the Islamic faith, responded positively to his campaign's promise of greater freedom and accountability by the government. The new language that Khatami's public pronouncements brought to political debate in Iran was a main pillar of his popularity. His call for building a civil society based on the rule of law, and his public defense of liberal-democratic virtues such as pluralism and tolerance, were indeed unprecedented for a cleric holding high office in Iran.

Another key reason for Khatami's popularity during his presidency was that, emboldened by his election, those religious intellectuals and journalists closely associated with him turned into the system's most vociferous critics inside Iran. Every time the conservative factions shut down a newspaper or magazine loyal to Khatami for being too loudly critical, every time they imprisoned or harassed the proponents of change who had arisen from within the ranks of the system itself, the forces of reform gained in legitimacy.

Khatami's book *Islam, Liberty and Development*, which was published in English in 1998, took a bold stand against religious dogma. He underscored the importance of freedom to the development process, the compatibility of reason and religion, and the necessity of transforming clerical rule in Iran so that it allows greater public participation and pluralism.

In line with the content of his book, Khatami's speech before eight hundred Iranian expatriates—who gathered at the United Nations to hear him the day before his address to the General Assembly in September 1998—was outstanding because of its emphasis on Iranian national identity. In response to a question from a Zoroastrian member of the audience, Khatami noted, "We were all Zoroastrians first," stressing the role of Persia's pre-Islamic past in shaping Iranian identity. For close to two decades most of the clerics who ruled Iran had tried to deny or downgrade the importance of the Iranian people's national identity, trying to supplant it with a pan-Islamic ideology. Khatami's pronouncements marked the beginning of a new era.

One of Khatami's favorite claims, which indicated the influence of Abdol-Karim Soroush—Iran's most noted religious intellectual—on his thinking, was that religious interpretation is dynamic and prone to change. Retrograde religiosity, Khatami suggested, was absolutely incapable of defending the sanctity of religion for it has no way of addressing the public demand for change. Equally important was his high regard for the achievements of the West, which he conceded is today's "predominant" global civilization, many of whose tenets Iranians and other Muslims have no choice but to internalize if they seek to embark on the path of development.

Throughout the 1990s, Soroush, in his voluminous writings, had mounted a powerful philosophical critique of religious despotism, and had helped lay the groundwork for the reformist victory in 1997. Well-versed in Islamic and western scholarship, Soroush, who had served in the controversial High Council for Cultural Revolution in the early 1980s, critiqued the harsh tactics of the ruling clerics by showing that Islam as a religion is compatible with democracy and popular sovereignty, and that the repression of free speech in Iran in the name of Islam was highly damaging to Islam and the country.

What gave Soroush legitimacy in Iran was his deep knowledge of Islam and the fact that he was a supporter of the revolution and a pious Muslim. By showing the incompatibility of Islam as a religion and totalitarianism as a political philosophy, Soroush mounted the most effective critique of clerical rule in Iran.

The following quotes from Soroush highlight the essence of his attempt to reform Islam as the governing ideology of the state:

> No one group of people has the exclusive right to interpret or reinterpret religion. That is something to be abolished. In Islam it is the right of all people to believe in Allah and in the Koran, and it follows then that they all have an equal right to their own justifiable understanding of Islam. No understanding of religion is considered the final or most complete understanding. There is no official interpretation. There should always be a plurality of interpretations. The [ideal] religious state should protect the conditions for this freedom. It is neither its right nor its duty to impose a particular understanding on the people. Religious interpretation is thus pluralistic in nature and this pluralism should be widened.[1]

In his writings, Soroush discussed the primacy of individuals in their relationship to God and to the government, even if the government was led by the clergy, who claimed to be God's representatives on earth. Thus, his work provides the most potent philosophical basis for separating mosque from state. Soroush's work shows that Islam does not provide a blueprint for modern governance. Thus, in Sorough's view, theocracy as a form of modern government cannot claim to be authentically anchored in Islamic tenets. While Soroush does not exclude the clergy from playing a role in government, he refutes their current privileged status, which in effect places them above the law.

> Religious ideology should not be used to rule a modern state for it tends toward totalitarianism. The use of religious ideology in governance also blocks the growth of religious knowledge. . . . In [an ideal] religious society, no personality and no *fatwa* [religious decree] is above criticism.[2]

The most significant political implication of Soroush's thinking is that it critiques the monopoly of power held by the office of the Supreme Jurist, which was created by Khomeini, and is now held by Khamenei. Similarly, he opposes the broad-based powers held by the twelve-member Guardian Council, accountable to the Supreme Leader. In short, Soroush's work has worked to undermine the use of Islam as the basis for dictatorship. In his thinking, no individual, including high-ranking clerics, can claim to be the sole interpreters of God's will. They certainly cannot legitimately use their religious credentials to govern.

Soroush's reformist thought, which was disseminated to tens of thousands of people through his popular lectures in universities and mosques across the country in the early to mid-1990s, provided the theoretical groundwork for the reform movement to succeed in electing Khatami to the presidency in 1997. His ideas had grown so popular that before the election, Soroush was banned from delivering lectures in public, and a strict injunction was imposed on his writings. In a few instances, Soroush was physically attacked by government-backed vigilantes who were taught to believe that Soroush was undermining Islam. Despite these restrictions, however, Soroush's work had been absorbed by the new generation of religious reformers, who remained loyal to the revolution's tenets, but wished to stem the tide of the state's drift toward autocracy.

The group of religious intellectuals who stood behind Khatami, also acting as his advisers in the world of ideas and public relations, bore the brunt of the conservative backlash. Resurrected by his election, these were the real "Khatami men" in the public eye. During the preceding two-term presidency of Rafsanjani (1989–1997) as the Iranian parliament was dominated by conservatives, they had been marginalized and sometimes imprisoned for their vocal criticism of the government's record on social justice.

Two who fit this description were Mashallah Shamsolvaezin and Hamid-Reza Jalaipour, who served as the editor and publisher of the pro-Khatami newspaper *Jameah* for six months until September 1998, when both men were taken into custody while the authorities shut down their newspaper for "abusing the freedom of speech." Jalaipour came from a religious family loyal to the revolution. His two brothers were killed in the war with Iraq in the 1980s, while he, too, served in the Revolutionary Guards during the war years. During a trial widely publicized by the paper itself, Jalaipour defended *Jameah*—which means "society"—by reminding the judges of the significance of the vote of Khordad the 2nd, and the necessity of heeding its demand for greater openness.

Upon *Jameah*'s publication in the spring of 1998, large advertisements painted on the walls of Tehran called it "Iran's first civil society newspaper." While civil society had gradually become a favorite topic of Iranian academics prior to Khatami's election, *Jameah*, which was printed in color, focused unprecedented attention on the importance to a healthy polity of civil debate, a culture of critique, and the freedom of speech. Soon after publication, the paper attracted a large readership, reaching a circulation of 300,000, and becoming the country's second most widely read newspaper almost overnight. Equally important was the quality of the paper's readership: young, progressive, and educated strata who did not wish Iran's future to resemble its past.

The author of a full-page article published by *Jameah* in June 1998, under the title "Religion, Freedom and Law," was a cleric living in Qum who expanded on Khatami's oft-quoted claim that "if religion goes against freedom it will lose." The headline of another June issue quoted Khatami's announcement to a gathering of Revolutionary Guards that "society cannot be moved forward by instilling fear."

Even more important were unprecedented references to the "national interest" on the front page of *Jameah* in the summer of 1998, a move that overturned close to two decades of prohibition against the expression of nationalist sentiment in the press. During the same period, in his first speech to a Washington audience, Iran's Ambassador to the United Nations, Hadi Nejad-Hosseinian, actually mentioned the name of Mohammad Mossadegh, the nationalist Iranian prime minister who was overthrown by a CIA-sponsored coup in 1953. Before Khatami's election no Iranian official dared acknowledge the contribution of nationalist leaders to advancing Iran's interests.

The May 23, 1998 issue of *Jameah*, celebrating the one-year anniversary of the Khatami victory, printed a large caption on the first page: superimposed on the middle white horizontal stripe of the green-white-red Iranian flag, in the place of the logo of the Islamic Republic, it read, "The rule of law is not the victory of any one person, but the great victory of all women and men in the Islamic land of Iran." The use of the word "land" indicated the nationalist leaning of many Khatami supporters.

Another pro-Khatami publication that emerged and was shut down in the summer of 1998 was the weekly *Rah-e No*, which means "New Way." A long piece in the July 23 issue featured pictures of Mossadegh, one of him in prison garb defiantly raising his arm in the courtroom. The summer of 1998 was the summer of trials in Tehran: the trial of the Mayor, Gholamhossein Karbaschi, the trial of Jalaipour, and the impeachment and removal of the pro-Khatami minister of interior, Abdollah Nouri. So the most intrepid of Khatami's supporters brought back the legacy of Mossadegh to the Iranian public sphere in an attempt to attract nationalists to their cause.

Rah-e No quoted Mossadegh:

> World politics will not allow time for our cabinet shuffles. We need a stable national policy. If the parliament allows the government to have confidence in its own longevity, there will be an opportunity to bring the country out of uncertainty. A good government, when it cannot last, will not succeed in any reforms. How can the minister who gives an order and a week later faces a non-confidence vote in the parliament have the courage to begin reforms? No nation has gotten anywhere under the shadow of autocracy; a dictator is similar to a father who distances his children from the environment of action and work, and after his death leaves behind inexperienced, incapable people in his place.

The lead story of *Jameah* on June 9, 1998, contained a large picture of Jalaipour; he too, had raised his arm in defiance in the courtroom. The complete text of his remarks to the head of the Press Court and the presiding jury also appeared in the paper. He ended his hour-long speech by saying,

> Respected jurors and the Press Court, I insist that *Jameah* is innocent of all that it has been accused of. *Jameah* is a small institution of civil society dedicated to the political development of Islamic Iran.

The pro-Khatami press also gave coverage to the misappropriation of public funds by officials. Late spring issues of *Jameah* published the entire translated text of an October 1997 IMF report on government corruption. While the report was a case study of Italy, it was intended to shed light on the situation in Iran:

Even a mere commission of a few percent in a plan whose implementation costs hundreds of millions of dollars is an astronomical amount that tempts many to do wrong. The politicians are very fond of ribbon-cutting ceremonies upon the completion of dams, roads, schools, and hospitals. The corruption of the system's top officials changes the plans . . .

It was worthy of note that the former statist ideologues of the Islamic revolution were quoting the IMF. A case in point was the prominent political columnist, Abbas Abdi, who wrote for *Rah-e No* during the brief period it was allowed to publish. Abdi had been among the leaders of the students loyal to Ayatollah Khomeini, who invaded and took over the U.S. embassy in Tehran in 1979. Abdi's appearance in Paris in late July 1998 to debate and shake hands with Barry Rosen, the former press attaché at the U.S. embassy who had spent over a year as a captive in Tehran, was a thinly disguised appeal of the Khatami faction for improving American-Iranian relations. The *New York Times* of August 1, 1998, quoted Abdi as saying (about the legacy of the hostage ordeal), "the past cannot be altered; instead we must focus on the years ahead and endeavor to build a better future." Abdi, too, drew inspiration from Mossadegh in his speech.

In his writings in the early 1990s, Abdi had opposed the merchants' pockets allied to the government for straying from the revolution's authentic, populist path, which had led to his imprisonment for eight months in 1993. After Khatami's election, Abdi enjoyed a higher public profile, disseminating his views more freely. He and like-minded intellectuals close to Khatami had a good reputation in Iran because they had not enriched themselves by misappropriating public funds, even though they had been deeply inside the system in the 1980s. Their attempt to project an image of being uninterested in personal wealth, which was often genuine, added to the public's trust in their motives. In the following years, Abdi and his colleagues conducted an opinion poll of Iranians' views on relations with the United States. Once the results showed that a significant majority of Iranians were in favor of restored relations with the United States, Abdi and his colleagues Hossein Ghazian and Behrooz Geranmayeh, were imprisoned for "undermining national security." Upon their release from prison, they have kept a low profile.

For the first three years of Khatami's presidency beginning in 1997, Iran experienced a period of openness that advanced the cause of political development and democracy in the country. Dozens of new publications sprouted across the country and discussed the necessity of fundamental reform in Iran's theocratic structure. Numerous religious intellectuals opined that while Khomeini's role had been indispensable in the revolution's victory, the country had to move beyond the Khomeini era in the 1980s and build a system attuned to the demands of the time.

Yet the era of political openness was short-lived. In February 2000, the re-formists allied to Khatami swept to power in the country's parliamentary elections. This victory provided the impetus for Germany's Heinrich Boll Foundation to organize a major conference of Iran's leading activists and intellectuals in Berlin, which was entitled "Iran after the elections." At the conference, which took place in early April 2000, noted activists such as Akbar Ganji, Mehrangiz Kar, and Ezatollah Sahabi mounted fundamental critiques of the system of religious rule in Iran and called for change in the system to reflect the public's demand for change. Upon returning to Iran from the conference, most of the participants at the Berlin conference were imprisoned for their pronouncements that, in the eyes of conservative judicial authorities, had undermined national security.

Coinciding with the imprisonment of outspoken critics, the judiciary moved to shut down dozens of newspapers who had become powerful vehicles for the expression of public opinion. With the mass closure of the newspapers, which Khatami was powerless to stop, the potential of Khatami's election to create a more open and tolerant system within the boundaries of the Islamic Republic became stillborn. The reformist phase in Iranian politics was forcibly brought to an end as the theocracy reverted to its old ways of repressing dissent, even if it came from religious intellectuals who had all been supporters of the revolution. Akbar Ganji was arguably the most significant voice who was imprisoned and remained in captivity for the following five years.

In the preceding three years, Ganji had become Iran's most popular investigative journalist by exposing the involvement of Iran's intelligence ministry in the murder of dozens of Iranian intellectuals within and outside the country. In his books, *The Red Eminence* and *The Dark House of Ghosts*, which appeared in rapid succession in the late 1990s, Ganji reprinted many of the columns he had published in the reformist press. Ganji's columns in *Sobh-e Emrooz* had been especially hard-hitting. *Sobh-e Emrooz* (which means "This Morning") was published by Saeed Hajjarian, a former intelligence official who had transformed himself into a leading advocate and strategist of the reform movement. It exposed the government's involvement in the serial murders of thinkers and dissidents. For his role in exposing these truths, Hajjarian became the victim of an assassination attempt in March 2000, which left him a quadriplegic.

In the year 2001, while in prison, Ganji authored his "Republican Manifesto," which took his call for reform to new heights. While the preceding reformists who hailed from religious backgrounds had sought to reform religious rule, Ganji sought a complete separation of religion and state in Iran. Ganji began his manifesto with a quote by Khomeini:

> Human rights means that every people must determine their own destiny. This means that now we must determine our own destiny. We have no right to determine the future of our successors. Succeeding generations come after us, which was [*sic*] must be in their own hands, not in ours.

With this note of approval from the revolution's founder, Ganji delved into discussing the need for instituting liberal democratic principles in Iran, based on free elections, a separation of mosque and state, as well as freedom of association and press. In such a system, in Ganji's view, religion has no place in the halls of power. He wrote:

A republican anthropology claims that there are no infallible individuals, and that all people are fully human, and thus fallible and possessed of this-worldly ambition. The constitution of a republic is designed precisely for controlling the autocratic tendencies of fallible and power-hungry individuals. This means that the principles of the republic must be so precise and transparent to prevent autocrats from using vague concepts to further their autocracy and corruption.

A modern republic is ideologically neutral. In such a republic the institution of religion is separated from the institution of government. This is based on the theory that neither can a religious government be called a government, nor a religion. A religious democracy is a paradox. The important point is that the government has no right to interfere in religion, while religion, similar to other social institutions, can critique the government . . . Thus, in a modern republic the government must be neutral toward religions, and not the defender of a specific religion.

Ganji's manifesto provides a theoretical model for the reform of political institutions in Iran. It is a powerful document that, along with his other writings, has made Ganji Iran's best-known dissident. Since his release from prison in 2005, Ganji has spent extended periods outside Iran, drawing large crowds of Iranian expatriates to his lectures in the United States, Canada, and Europe. He has given interviews to dozens of international broadcasters, and has lectured at dozens of universities, and at one of the main think tanks of the U.S. foreign policy establishment, the Council on Foreign Relations in New York. His main vision is to help bring about a full-fledged republic in Iran, which is based on liberal democratic tenets. As an observant Muslim, similar to those we surveyed above, Ganji is concerned that under a theocracy any deficiency and injustice in government will in time come to be seen as a deficiency of Islam. Thus, he worries that a government that rules in the name of Islam will inadvertently turn people away from religion. The high respect that Ganji has shown in his writings and letters toward Abdolkarim Soroush, whom he calls his "professor," and toward Hossein-Ali Montazeri, the country's leading clerical dissident who lives under house arrest in the city of Najafabad in central Iran, show Ganji's high regard for religious reformers.

In his writings, Ganji has displayed his familiarity with western philosophers ranging from Kant and Neitzche to Giddens and Habermas. He has played an invaluable role in making the philosophical underpinnings of liberal democracy comprehensible to the tens of thousands of loyal readers that his writings have found across Iran. Ganji's work represents the natural progression of religious reformist thinking that was begun by Soroush after the revolution, found political expression under Khatami, and has now reached its pinnacle with Ganji. What began as an attempt to make Islam compatible with democracy in Iran has reached a stage where Islam is viewed as secondary to the Iranian people's wish for basic freedoms and security from the arbitrary exercise of power. It is indeed worthy of note that the most trenchant critiques of Iran's theocracy have come from people such as Soroush, Abdi, Hajjarian, and Ganji, all of whom have impeccable revolutionary credentials. They have performed this task far more successfully than could be expected from secular thinkers and activists, for they have utilized religious discourse to critique what they see as the current opposition of the official version of Islam with the demands of democracy.

The main shortcoming of the discourse of religious intellectuals is their insufficient attention to the issues of political economy and political culture in Iran. Their guidelines offer respectable ideals for Iran, without spelling out in any detail how the country's government can be reformed to empower Iranians to build better lives for themselves and their children. Similarly, while these religious intellectuals have indeed taken the time to gain familiarity with the philosophical tenets of liberal democracy in the West, they have not discussed the cultural and economic underpinnings of democracy. Nor have they paid sufficient attention to the need for political institution building to regulate the political activities of Iranians. With the thirtieth anniversary of the revolution approaching, Iran still lacks political parties in the traditional sense. A cacophony of amorphous factions dot the Iranian political landscape, none of which have proposed a cohesive platform that can address the main challenges facing the country. This is a task that must be accomplished by Iranians within the country who wish to avoid the equally harmful extremes of autocracy and chaos. In today's environment in Iran, if complete freedom were provided to the country's political factions, many dozens of political parties would come into being almost overnight, and the country would be sunk into a state of chaos. To control such chaos, the government would once again be left with no recourse other than to terrorize the population and suppress all dissent.

The key challenge of crafting a political philosophy that can bring order, freedom, and progress to Iran's landscape is a nationwide discourse that is based on tolerance, and on the primacy of the national interest. The main focus of such a movement needs to be promoting peace among various leanings, religious and secular, nationalist and liberal. In the years ahead it is crucial to instill in the population a respect for diversity, under a developmental and democratic umbrella. Iranians' best hope for a better future is to break the vicious cycle of violence that has marred their political life in the pre- and postrevolutionary periods alike.

At the same time, in charting their path toward the future, Iranians must realize that no system of government, no matter how progressive and democratic, can bring development to the country unless the people themselves adopt democratic virtues. In this area, especially, the discourse of religious reformists remains deficient. The most acute need Iran faces, more acute than sudden and unpredictable changes in the system of government, is a program of public education that can focus on the cultural and participatory underpinnings of development and progress, and orderly social behavior. Indeed, in a country where the rules of social conduct border on perpetual chaos, evident as we noted above in the tens of thousands of people who are killed on the country's roads every year, discussions of western philosophical traditions, while necessary, are by no means sufficient. For far too long, Iranians have expected their government to deliver progress and national development from above. Political and cultural institution building at the grassroots level is a national necessity. The key attributes of such institution building must be the promotion of tolerance and inclusiveness, and the means of effective group work that has eluded Iranians to date.

DIVERSITY AND MULTICULTURALISM IN IRAN

One of the distinguishing features of Iran is the pluralistic nature of its society, which has a religious and an ethnolinguistic dimension. Its religious diversity spans Christians, Jews, Zoroastrians, and Bahais, whose combined numbers approach one million people in Iran. The largest of these religious minorities are the Armenian community who number over 250,000 people and are concentrated in Tehran, Isfahan, Shiraz, and Tabriz. In her book, *Religious Minorities in Iran*, Eliz Sanasarian provides a comprehensive look at the restrictions faced by Iran's religious minorities in the postrevolutionary period. Since the constitution of the Islamic Republic gives the majority Muslim population primacy over members of other religions, the path for gaining their full citizenship rights has been arduous for them. She discusses the continuing restrictions placed on religious minorities in teaching their faiths to their children in public schools.

The Armenian community have practiced their faith in the historical boundaries of Iran for as long has they have been Christian: for over seventeen centuries. They have thus been deeply integrated into Iranian society. More so than in most other countries in the Middle East, Armenians in Iran have continued their religious practices largely uninterrupted for most of their recorded history and have made major contributions to the development of a pluralistic Iranian culture over the centuries. The most monumental of the Armenian churches in the country, in the Jolfa district of Isfahan, were built under the reign of Shah Abbas in the early seventeenth century, and later in Shiraz. The Armenian community has two deputies in the Iranian parliament. While state funds for the promotion of Armenian language and culture are limited, the community itself is among the most active in transferring their culture to future generations.[3]

The Jewish community of Iran, similarly, has an ancient history in the country. From the time of the birth of the Persian Empire under Cyrus the Great, who freed them from Babylonian captivity over twenty-five centuries ago—and is mentioned on numerous occasions in the Old Testament as a saint—the Jewish people have had a presence in Iran. Their community especially flourished in the Pahlavi era and numbered close to 150,000 people. After the revolution the majority of Iranian Jews left the country for Israel or the United States. The close to 30,000 Jews who remain in Iran, however, still constitute the largest Jewish community in any Muslim country. Iran has more synagogues than any country in the Middle East, except Israel itself. Scores of ancient synagogues and Jewish monuments dot the architectural landscape of the country and span the country's regions. Instances of violence or desecration of these monuments have been extremely rare in Iran, even during the revolutionary fervor of the 1980s. The Jewish community has one representative in the Iranian parliament.

The most controversial issue regarding Iran's treatment of its religious minorities pertains to the adherents of the Bahai faith. Bahaism came into existence in Iran in the mid-nineteenth century, and was introduced to adherents in dozens of other countries in the late nineteenth and early twentieth centuries. Bahaism was created through the influence of Shaikhism and the related Babism. Shaikhism was a sect of Shia Islam that, in the 1830s and 1840s, preached that the Hidden Imam was to return in 1844. Babism grew out of Shaikism, but departed from it when its leader, Ali Mohammad Shirzai (1819–1850) also known as Bab, declared that he was the representative of the Hidden Imam. The Qajar state in Iran, acting upon the clerical establishment's charges of heresy against Bab, executed him and other leaders in the Babist community. What is today known as Bahaism came from Babism. Mirza Hossein-Ali Nouri (1817–1892), also known as Bahaullah, made a declaration in 1860 that he was the divine manifestation of God, and the messianic figure whose rise had been predicted by Bab. Bahaullah was condemned by the Iranian and Ottoman states and clergymen, and he fled in the final years of his life to Palestine, where he died.[4]

While based on a doctrine of international peace and brotherhood, whose purview is international, the Bahai faith has been controversial in Iran since its inception because it is based on the philosophy of "progressive revelation," which means that God continually sends new prophets to enlighten humans. This tenet of Bahaism is viewed as clashing with Islam's view of itself as the last Godly religion. Thus, while the Islamic Republic sees Jews, Christians, and Zoroastrians, as "people of the book," it has not accorded this status to Bahais. Thus, Bahais, unlike other religious minorities, have not been allowed to practice their religion publicly. Nor have they been allowed representation in the Iranian parliament. Scores of prominent Bahais were executed or imprisoned in the first decade after the revolution of 1979. Their community, numbering hundreds of thousands of people in Iran—this is an estimate since Bahais are not allowed to declare their religion in the national census—lives in a state of denial and suppression. A more tolerant and inclusive government in Iran will have to broaden opportunities for religious expression and allow members of all faiths, including the Bahai, to live and worship in peace.

Among Iran's population of 70 million, whose official state language is Persian, over one third, close to 25 million people, speak Azeri-Turkish as a mother tongue. Similarly, though in lesser numbers, Kurdish, Baluchi, and Arabic, when taken as a whole, are spoken by millions of Iranians.

The distinguishing feature of the two most significant ethnic minorities in Iran, the Azeris and the Kurds, is their deep attachment to Iranian identity. The Kurdish people have for millennia lived on the Iranian plateau, and their language and customs, from celebrations of Nowruz (the Iranian New Year) to the ancient Zoroastrian festival of fire, bear distinct marks of their attachment to Iranian identity. For this reason, especially, Iranian Kurds have felt secure in their place in Iran. The Turkic population of Iran, similarly, concentrated in the country's north-western and north-eastern regions, have made seminal contributions, over many centuries, to the construction of Iranian identity.[5]

Since Reza Shah's time, public schools in the Iranian provinces of Azerbaijan and Kurdistan have not been allowed to teach in the local languages of Turkish and Kurdish, delivering their curriculum entirely in Persian. Despite the hardships this policy had caused these two communities, it has worked to further deepen their integration into the country's national identity. In current circumstances, with its national unity on a solid footing, Iran is in a position to consider granting more schooling language rights to these communities, provided their spoken and written fluency in Persian is not compromised. Once they are secure in their place in the national family, Iranian Azeris and Kurds—if Iran invests in their human and cultural capital—can act as goodwill ambassadors and trade representatives of Iran in countries where their mother tongues are spoken, especially in Turkey, and in Iraq, where the Kurdish minority has gained autonomy after the American-led invasion of the country in 2003.

With the newfound autonomy of the Kurds in Iraq, the governments in Turkey, Syria, and to a lesser extent Iran, are worried that if the Kurdish people of Iraq declare official autonomy and establish a country called Kurdistan, their respective Kurdish populations may make similar demands and thus threaten the territorial integrity of these countries. Iran is ideally positioned to promote peaceful conflict resolution between the Kurds and the governments of their respective host countries. Because of its tradition of multiethnic and multireligious tolerance, Iran is well positioned to fulfill this role.

While the pre- and postrevolutionary governments in Iran had justifiably worried about the centrifugal tendencies that might be unleashed across the country if a multitude of customs, religions, and languages are allowed to flourish, Iran has reached a stage in its national development where its diversity can now be harnessed as a source of strength. By empowering its ethnic and religious minorities to practice their customs in peace and freedom, Iran is uniquely positioned to share its experiences with other countries in the region.

WOMEN'S RIGHTS

One of the key areas in which the Iranian clergy failed to honor their promises has been the Islamic Republic's treatment of women. Beginning in the early 1980s, having decimated their political opponents, the clergy began clamping down on women's rights by instituting mandatory veiling, which meant that not covering their hair became a criminal offense for the women of Iran. Throughout the 1980s and 1990s, the government-sanctioned moral police roamed the streets of Iran's cities in search of moral "vice." Their tactics of humiliating the country's youth were especially directed at young women who were habitually rounded up and taken into custody for attending parties and associating with men, with whom they were not legally related. During this time, morality police made a habit of invading the private sanctity of the homes of Iranians and created an environment of fear across the country. The simple pleasures of socialization were deemed as un-Islamic, and the country's youth were left in the hands of the moral police, who were among the least educated strata of society. The humiliation of the country's youth was practiced through the beating and lashing of moral infractors. The irony of these practices is that drug addiction and other vices have reached record levels in postrevolutionary Iran.

Yet the invasion of the civil liberties of Iranians by the cleric-led government was not limited to the country's adventurous urban youth. Even more significant was the systematic downgrading of women's rights in postrevolutionary Iran. To be sure, under the two-term presidencies of Rafsanjani and Khatami, women's rights, and civil freedoms more generally, improved noticeably. But the harsh precedent set in the 1980s, and the record of meting out "Islamic justice" has been difficult to erase.

One of the best books on the concerns of women after the revolution is Haleh Esfandiari's *Reconstructed Lives: Women and Iran's Islamic Revolution.* Esfandiari, an Iranian-American scholar, was the deputy director for the Iranian Women's Organization in Mohammad Reza Shah's time, and focused on civil and human rights issues in Iran after the revolution. She writes:

> Women from all classes were participants in the events leading to the overthrow of the monarchy in 1979. They joined the revolutionary movement for a variety of reasons—religious and secular, economic and political, conservative, moderate, and radical. But the vast majority of women expected the revolution to lead to an expansion, not a contraction, of their rights and opportunities. They did not expect that the gains they had made in the previous five decades would be put on hold or reversed. They did not anticipate men would once again secure the right to divorce their wives on demand or that women would need the permission of their spouses to work. They did not imagine they would find themselves unwelcome at their places of work, that a new penal code would impose special punishments on women, or that they would lose the right to choose what they wore. They did not foresee that a society segregated on the basis of sex was in the making . . . But women very soon discovered that the Islamic regime had its own women's agenda and that this agenda was not in keeping with promises that had been made to them. The state arrogated to itself the right to determine what jobs women could hold, what subjects they could study, how they should dress and behave in public, and how they should relate to men. Imagining women primarily as mothers, spouses, and homemakers, the state attempted to set procreation policy. It discouraged birth control and instructed women to bear more children.[6]

As this quote shows, the Islamic government suspended some of the key laws on women's rights, especially in the domain of personal and family law, which had been enacted during the former regime. Women were pressured to leave government jobs and they were purged from decision-making positions. Segregation of sexes was imposed in public places, and in schools. Islamic dress codes were enforced and violators faced brutal flogging. A woman out with a man in a car, on the street, or in a restaurant could be stopped by revolutionary committees or the morals police and asked to show proof that she was related by blood or by marriage to her male companion. Failure to do so brought harsh punishment ranging from imprisonment, fines, and flogging. Women were told that their bodies were sin-provoking.

Members of the revolutionary committees were free to enter anyone's home at will to ensure compliance with Islamic standards. Untold numbers of people faced the trauma of their doors being broken down by morals police who would arrest and take away people from their homes on charges of watching movies, listening to music, or entertaining guests. The reign of terror was especially acute in this area as the sanctity of the home was overlooked in the 1980s.[7]

Yet these government policies failed. The clerics contributed unwittingly to the propelling of women into the public sphere. While the veil was a hindrance to secular strata, it emboldened women of more traditional backgrounds to integrate fully into national institutions, and stake their claim among the country's professional classes. The clergy had called on women to take part in anti-Shah demonstrations, and women had responded. After the revolution, it was difficult to take away rights that they had enjoyed in the previous regime and throughout the revolution. That is why the clergy resorted to heavy-handed tactics.

The revolution, by involving millions of women in a transformative national exercise, had given them a keener sense of their rights. This movement is not limited to urban and secular strata and has become widespread among women of all backgrounds. In the Pahlavi era there was a schism between urban, modern women and others. Yet after the revolution a greater integration has been achieved inadvertently, not only among different classes of women, but among urban and rural Iranians more broadly.[8]

The first nationwide election in which women voted in Iran was held in 1963. In that election six women were elected to the country's parliament. This was followed, in 1967, by the landmark Family Protection Law, which aimed to create parity between men and women in child custody, divorce, and marriage cases. It placed legal obstacles in the way of polygamy, which had been steadily declining in Iran throughout the Pahlavi era. As far as women were concerned, this legislation was one of the most progressive that had arisen in Muslim countries. Amendments were made to the 1967 law in 1975, which assigned custody of children to the mother in case of the father's death, and raised the age of marriage for women to eighteen. Prior to this landmark legislation, women could be married off at puberty, and custody of children was reserved for male members of the father's families, in case of the father's death.[9]

On the eve of the revolution of 1979, Iranian women were serving as ministers and deputy ministers in the cabinet, and as ambassadors to foreign countries. Women sat as judges in the courts. They made major strides in the professions. They taught at all levels from kindergarten to university. They also served in the military and as traffic police. In rural areas, tens of thousands of young women served the country as members of the Literacy Corps or Health Corps. In 1978, over 2 million Iranian women were in the labor force. There were more than 150,000 women in the civil service. More than 1,500 women held managerial positions. The number of women deputies in parliament had reached twenty-two; more than 330 women served on local councils. There were five women mayors. Thirty-three percent of all seats in higher education were occupied by women.[10]

With these advances, the hundreds of thousands of women who demonstrated against the Shah's regime on the streets of the country's largest cities, could not imagine that the coming to power of a theocracy would be at their expense. They did not expect that the new theocracy was focused on turning the clock back as far as their hard-won rights were concerned. Khomeini has declared from exile on numerous occasions that Islam respected women's rights.

When the revolution succeeded, the new authorities immediately targeted women's rights: the Family Protection Law's provisions were overturned, the veil was made mandatory, and for the small number of women left in government positions, the dress code became the head-to-toe black chador. The new constitution, which was ratified in December 1979, devoted only four of 175 articles to women, and these articles focused on the role of women in the family, and within the context of Islamic law and traditions. To be sure, women kept the right to vote, to be elected to parliament, and to hold positions as cabinet ministers. However, the constitution barred women from being judges, or serving as the country's supreme religious leader, which was reserved for the country's senior male clerics.[11] The same can be said about the office of president, as the term "rejal" is used in the constitution, which means "men."

The minimum age for marrying girls was reduced to puberty, consistent with Islamic principles. The execution of the former minister of education, Farrokhru Parsa, on charges of spreading vice and prostitution, was one of the most savage acts of the revolutionary government. Parsa had been the first woman minister in Iranian history. Her execution showed the disdain with which the ruling clerics viewed the human rights of women.[12]

In response to these new restrictions, women fought for the restoration of their rights. The new regime soon realized that some policies of the old regime—such as family planning—were dictated by economic necessity and common sense, and that their abolishment would bring about catastrophic results. The new regime also saw that the public would not tolerate Islamic punishments such as stoning and flogging. Having experienced education and employment opportunities, legal protections, and a degree of freedom in dress and lifestyle before the revolution, women from all strata refused to be cowed. This same logic was at work regarding family planning and birth control, which went through a complete about-face after the 1980s.

Despite the significant progress made by women in demanding their rights in response to the postrevolutionary curtailment of those rights women are still second-class citizens in Iran. Most of the progress embodied in the Family Protection Law of the Pahlavi era has been erased.

One of the leading proponents of women's rights in contemporary Iran is Mehrangiz Kar, who has lived outside Iran since 2001, after being released from prison in Tehran. She is currently a scholar in residence at the Harvard Law School. On improving women's legal rights and numerous other contentious issues in the Islamic Republic, Kar's voice is arguably the most poignant of a generation. For over three decades, before and after the revolution of 1979, Kar's essays, books, and her litigation of difficult cases as a lead attorney in Iranian courts, have helped place the issue of women's changing roles and human rights in Iran on the public agenda—first within Iran itself, then beyond. Kar's career in Iran as an advocate of progressive causes reached a crescendo during the reform period of the late 1990s, when her seminal, multivolume works on violence against women and legal obstacles to reform in Iran were published to extensive acclaim. Kar has also been a leader in the establishment of women's studies as an academic discipline in Iran.

In April 2000, after her moving speech to the "Berlin conference," Kar achieved international prominence. As noted above, she and sixteen colleagues among Iran's leading activists and public intellectuals had been invited by the German Green Party's Heinrich Boll Foundation to a major conference in Berlin entitled "Iran after the Elections." The conference was broadcast to millions in Persian through shortwave radio and satellite TV. It established Kar as one of the most seasoned and energetic of Iran's embattled intelligentsia and, for being elected impromptu to inaugurate the Berlin conference, as one of the most articulate voices for reform. Following her speech in Berlin, where she posed fundamental legal challenges to the judicial system in Iran, Kar and colleagues returned to Iran and were arrested on charges of undermining the Iranian government. The publisher of Kar's works, Shahla Lahiji, another woman participant at the Berlin conference, was also arrested. Kar endured two months' imprisonment, much of it in solitary confinement, and was released upon intense pressure from the international community, led by Holland.[13]

Kar has worked tirelessly in bringing the plight of Iranian women to the world's attention. Kar's former colleague, Shirin Ebadi, who won the Nobel Peace Prize in 2003, has also been active inside and outside Iran in promoting women's rights. Despite their work and the efforts of dozens of their colleagues, the harsh treatment of women's rights activists has continued in Iran. On March 8, 2005 and 2006, especially, the Women's Day protests in Tehran were broken up by security forces, and dozens of women were detained for their activism.

Kar's uniqueness can be seen in the richness and depth of her scholarship and activism. It is also evident in her unshakable commitment to human rights and the freedom of speech. In the early 1960s, Kar had gained acceptance to the Faculty of Law and Political Science at the University of Tehran, the leading centre for the study of social sciences in Iran. Upon completing her studies in 1967, Kar was employed by the Social Welfare Organization of Iran. For the following twelve years until the revolution of 1979, she worked in numerous civil service positions, focused on the protection of women and families. She also became a noted essayist and columnist. Most noteworthy were her contributions to *Ferdowsi Magazine*, which was Iran's most important forum for social and political discourse in the prerevolutionary period. In recognition of her contributions to arts and letters, Kar was awarded the Forough Farrokhzad Award in 1975.

Kar had just passed the bar exam when the revolution instilled a new, religious system of government in Iran. Having been a part of the women's movement during the secularization drive of the Pahlavi era, Kar did not allow the newly imposed restrictions on women to hold her back. While many in her generation sought safer abodes abroad, Kar remained in Iran and, observing compulsory veiling in the workplace and in public, she took the judicial authorities to task based on their own laws. Few people in or outside Iran are in as good a position to help Iranians and the international community understand and reform Sharia-based legal systems.

The struggle of Iranian women for equal rights is inseparable from the democratic yearnings of the population more generally. The curtailment of their rights by the Iranian government projects a negative image of Iran in the international community. While the progress women have made since the early years of the revolution is unmistakable, their path toward full equality is likely to be long and arduous. Despite these difficulties, the issue of women's rights in Iran can no longer be seen as separate from human rights more generally.

In this chapter, we have examined the issues of religion and state in Iran, diversity and multiculturalism in the country, as well as women's rights under a theocratic system. The importance of these issues in the debate over the place of Iran in the international community is that the excesses of religious rule have portrayed Iranians as a backward and fanatical people in international forums, despite the fact that the majority of Iranians, similar to other peoples, are not ideologically blinded extremists. Any attempt at improving Iran's standing in international forums must address these and related issues.

Conclusion

THE DIALECTIC OF INDEPENDENCE AND INTERDEPENDENCE

For Iran and for many other developing countries the main challenge of foreign policy making will be to strike a healthy balance between independence and interdependence. One of the key slogans of Iranian revolutionaries in the late 1970s was "Independence, Freedom, Islamic Republic." They were right in assuming that without autonomy, states in the developing world cannot aim to improve their people's lot. Without having effective control over their own national policies, without being authentically anchored in their own national traditions, governments in the developing world will not have legitimacy in the eyes of their own people, which makes the drive for development, always an interactive process between the state and the people, far less steady and stable. At the same time, however, without effective interdependence with the industrialized world, and the sources of global capital, the technological and economic development of countries in the global south will be significantly set back. The success of China and India over the last quarter century in lifting hundreds of millions of people out of poverty is based in significant measure on their leaders' successful realization of this fact.

In the case of Iran, in particular, successful development will require achieving a dynamic balance between a nationalist—meaning independent—and liberal—meaning open—foreign policy. The first is related to Iran's need for building a domestically anchored and popular foreign policy, while the second is a key requirement of a globalized world in which national borders have been loosened at the hands of information and other technologies and the flow of global capital. To achieve this balance, Iran must overcome the ideological rigidity that has closed the doors of the country's foreign policy apparatus to all well-meaning Iranians who do not share all of the clerical hierarchy's rigid views of Iran's place among the community of nations, cast in opposition to the United States and its allies. Since the revolution of 1979, being a devout Muslim with familial ties to the clerical establishment in Iran has superseded professional knowledge of international affairs in the selection of those who represent the country abroad. An ideological litmus test has, with a few important exceptions, trumped actual knowledge of international affairs. Only then can Iran hope to become a bridge between East and West, between Muslim and non-Muslim, for which history and geography seem to have destined it. The current and future architects of Iran's foreign policy are likely to reap the benefits of modern bureaucratic development far more than their forebears did.

BREAKING THROUGH THE U.S.-IRAN DEADLOCK

For the first time in its postrevolutionary history, the Iranian leadership is unanimous in its wish for diplomatic negotiations with the United States. While this trend began during Rafsanjani's second term, and gained further momentum under Khatami, Ahmadinejad's presidency marks the first time that all political factions in Iran are in favor of breaking through a deadlock that has marred Iran's international relations since radicals climbed the walls of the U.S. embassy on November 4, 1980. Since coming to office, Ahmadinejad and his ultimate boss, Khamenei, have said repeatedly that "Iran is open to dialogue with *all* countries." And in late March 2006, Khamenei, for the first time since the revolution, made the unprecedented public announcement in Mashhad that he had no objections to negotiations with the United States.

Despite Iran's overtures, however, the mood in Washington has generally not been amenable to dialogue, mostly because the United States feels that by negotiating with Iran it will legitimize and give a new lease of life to a regime it has seen as America's adversary for close to three decades. The assumption in the Bush administration seems to be that with enough pressure, and the threat of military strikes against Iran, the Islamic Republic will unravel and a new, pro-American system of government will emerge in Iran. This is despite the fact that America's European and regional allies, with one or two exceptions, and the secretary general of the UN have all counseled Washington to open official negotiations with Iran, hoping for a diplomatic solution to the deadlock between the two countries over Iran's nuclear program. Similarly, eminent American foreign policy thinkers such as Madeleine Albright, Sandy Berger, and Dennis Ross, as well as Senator Chuck Hagel and many others have counseled the Bush administration to take up Iran's offer of negotiations to resolve lingering disputes between the two countries.[1] The Bush team, however, has shown little willingness to do so. The former U.S. ambassador to the U.N., John Bolton, is on record as claiming that "the US has nothing to say to Iran."

Throughout the 1990s and extending to the present, the United States, pursuing its policy of containing and isolating Iran, has opposed the expansion of Iranian diplomatic, trade and investment relations in the region that surrounds it, a policy that has yet to show any signs of abating. It seems as though U.S. policymakers still cannot accept, seventeen years after Khomeini's passing, the reality of the transformation of Iranian foreign policy to one that is driven by national interest calculations, one that has matured enough to function mostly independently of the specific government that is in power at any given time in Tehran. The foreign policy of Iran, building on the achievements of the Pahlavi era, has displayed remarkable continuity during the Rafsanjani, Khatami, and now, Ahmadinejad administrations. There are two main reasons for this continuity, one internal to Iran, one external.

In the wake of over seven decades of extensive bureaucratic development in Iran—from Reza Shah's time to the present—a modern foreign policy apparatus has matured in the country that, similar to all modern bureaucracies, is driven by its own rational calculus, as opposed to revolutionary and otherworldly concerns. This, as Max Weber showed, is the inescapable nature of modern bureaucracies.

The external reason for the emergence of an assertive, national interest-based foreign policy in Iran is the current international environment. At the time of the Iranian revolution, the global distribution of power was far less fluid, and far more predictable and certain than it is today. The emergence of China as a world power in the past quarter century; the expanding power of Russia and India; the advent of the eurozone encompassing over 400 million people, which, for the first time in postwar history has emerged as a viable competitor to the U.S. dollar; the rise of antiglobalization movements on all continents; Islamic political movements from Egypt to Indonesia; dwindling U.S. popularity across the world—these and many other new realities have created an international environment and a balance of power in the international arena that are, on the whole, favorable to regional powers such as Iran and Turkey who have a chance to create a balance of power of their own to be able to deliver security and development for their citizens.

If the United States joins this march, it has the potential, as it did after World War II, to once again become the champion of democracy and development on all continents. It was, after all, American leadership that ensured that the twentieth century did not become the century of Fascist or Communist totalitarianism. At the end of the "American Century" there were more democracies on the map, with more people lifted out of poverty with the help of American technology and inventiveness than would have been the case without America's indispensable leadership role. In Iran's particular case, one can argue that the country's drive for modernization and development would have been significantly set back without the relationship the country enjoyed with the United States throughout most of the last century. The reestablishment of diplomatic relations between Iran and the United States will not only be good for the two countries, but for many other countries as well. Instability in Iran and the region that surrounds it benefit no country, as they run the risk of unleashing forces that are in the control of no government or group of governments. Terrorism is indeed a scourge that knows no national borders.

The main point to remember for the United States regarding Iran is that irrespective of what kind of government comes to power there, Iranian foreign policy will be shaped by national interest calculations, which will be largely independent of electoral politics. Thus, it will be important for the United States to support the continued evolution of state institutions in Iran that can bring stability to the country itself and the region that surrounds it.

For Iranian policymakers interested in sowing the seeds of progress in Iran, it is necessary to create an environment of freedom and security so thinking can flourish about the ways in which the main obstacles in the way of the country's development can be tackled, and how the most important opportunities can be harnessed both within the country and abroad. Viewed in this light, the four-month incarceration of the Iranian-Canadian philosopher Ramin Jahanbegloo from April to August 2006, and most recently, the arrest of the Iranian-American scholars Haleh Esfandiari and Kian Tajbakhsh who have spent over four months in captivity at Tehran's notorious Evin Prison, show that the Iranian government must fundamentally reform the way it treats internationally minded scholars and activists who work on building cultural and intellectual bridges between Iran and other countries. Just as Jahanbegloo's arrest led to pleas for his release from eminent personalities in Canada, the United States and elsewhere, so too have Esfandiari and Tajabkhsh's detention been condemned by dozens of American and other lawmakers, scholars, and the Iranian Nobel Laureate Shirin Ebadi.[2]

The imprisonments of Jahanbegloo, Esfandiari, and Tajbakhsh show that the Iranian government is still not ready to embrace an inclusive vision of Iran in which a broad array of philosophies can coexist in harmony within the laws of the country. It shows that the Iranian government's main challenge remains overcoming the reactionary aspects of the 1979 revolution's legacy.

* * *

On May 28, 2007, the United States and Iran ended a twenty-seven-year freeze and held official bilateral negotiations in Baghdad over Iraq. The negotiations, which lasted four hours, were led by the American and Iranian ambassadors to Iraq, Ryan Crocker and Hassan Kazemi-Ghomi respectively.[3] According to Crocker, a broad policy consensus emerged between the United States and Iran over laying the groundwork for the emergence of a stable, democratic, and federal Iraq. These talks are highly significant as they are the first official and public exchange between the two countries since diplomatic relations were broken off in 1980. This is welcome news because the United States and Iran must revisit their policies—regarding each other and beyond—to bring greater stability and progress to the region that surrounds Iran. For both of them, in varying degrees, knowledge-intensive policy development offers the best antidote for reactionary and ideologically rigid views.

The restoration of diplomatic relations between the United States and Iran, if built on a solid footing of mutual respect, can have a powerful stabilizing effect on the region that surrounds Iran. As that eventuality approaches, we can only hope that all parties learn from the successes and failures of the past, and that they bring knowledge and courage to their attempts at building a better future.

Notes

INTRODUCTION

1. Brzezinski, Zbigniew. 1997. *The Grand Chessboard: American Primacy and Its Geostrategic Imperatives.* New York: Basic Books; Brzezinski, Zbigniew. 2004. *The Choice: Global Domination or Global Leadership.* New York: Basic Books.

2. Ibid., p. viii.

3. Ibid., p. 53.

4. Brzezinski, *The Choice*, pp. 73–75.

CHAPTER ONE

1. The most authoritative and updated book on Iran's constitutional revolution is the book by Janet Afary, *The Iranian Constitutional Revolution, 1906–1911*, Columbia University Press, 1996. This 448-page book is the most comprehensive account of the constitutional revolution available in print. The book uniquely demonstrates that the constitutional revolution was not just a political revolution through which one set of elites and one system of government replaced another, but, even more importantly, a social and cultural revolution in which a modern public sphere held up by a flourishing of newspapers, constitutional government and parliamentary democracy, and women's participation in public affairs, came to Iran, much of it for the first time. This source is distinguished for having a timeline of the constitutional revolution, which is very helpful since the revolution was so eventful, with innumerable personalities playing various roles, that it is easy to get overwhelmed as readers try to understand it. The other main source for understanding the Constitutional Revolution is the entries on the subject in *Encyclopedia Iranica*: entries on Constitutional Revolution are in pp. 163–220. This resource contains a great deal of information on the events of the revolution, the intellectual background, the press, and the role of political parties. Its various contributors include: Abbas Amanat, Vanessa Martin, and most importantly, for the sections on the political parties and the aftermath of the revolution, Mansoureh Ettehadieh. This can be seen full-text at www.iranica.com under "entries." Apart from these two sources, one can consult the first book on that revolution, written by the British historian,

activist, and man of letters Edward G. Browne, and which appeared in 1911 under the title, *The Persian Revolution of 1906–1909*. Other important references on Iranian society and politics—all in Persian—at this time include the works of Mohammad-Taqi Bahar, Ahmad Kasravi, and Mehdi Malekzadeh. It is worthy of note, however, that the first comprehensive account of Iran's first modern revolution was not provided by Iranians themselves, but by a sympathetic Englishman.

2. *Encyclopedia Iranica*, p. 180.

3. Taghizadeh's long life—he died at the age of 92 in Tehran in 1969—was deeply enmeshed with the political and cultural transformation of Iran into a modern nation throughout the twentieth century. Taghizadeh played a lead role during the years of the constitutional movement, and then served as governor, minister, and ambassador under both Pahlavi shahs, while making major contributions to Iranian studies internationally. Fluent in numerous regional and international languages, he had changed his turban for a suit and tie early in his life, and counts as one of the leading scholar-statesman of twentieth-century Iran. His autobiography, which appeared in the last years of his life in Persian, was aptly titled *Zendegiy-e Toufani*, which means "a stormy life." There is also a comprehensive biography of him available online at wikipedia.org.

4. Touraj Atabaki, ed. *Iran and the First World War: A Battleground of the Great Powers*. London: I.B.Tauris, 2006, pp. 1–5.

5. Mohammad Gholi Majid, *The Great Famine and Genocide in Persia*. Lanham, MD: University Press of America, 2003.

6. Ibid., pp. 1–10.

7. Mohammad Gholi Majd, *Persia in World War I and Its Conquest by Great Britain*. Landam, MD: University Press of America, 2003.

8. This section mostly draws on the following two biographies of Reza Shah, which are available in Persian: Agheli, Bagher. *Reza Shah va Ghoshoon-e Mottahedolshekl* (*Reza Shah and a Unified Army*). Tehran: Namak Publishers, 1998; Pesyan, Najafgholi *Az Savadkuh ta Zhuhanisburg* (*From Savadkooh to Johannesburg: The Story of Reza Khan*). Tehran: Main Publishers, 1999. Also consulted is Toloui, Mahmoud. *Pedar va Pessar: NaGofteha az Zengegi va Ruzegar-e Pahlaviha* (*Father and Son: The Untold Story of the Pahlavis*). Tehran: Nashre-Elm, 1995.

9. Most of the information here is gleaned from www.iranica.com.

10. This section draws from the Library of Congress country study on Iran, and the *Cambridge History of Iran*, as well as the books, in Persian, of Abdolreza Hooshang Mahdavi. See, especially, his 600-page *Siasat-e Khareji-e Iran Dar Doran-e Pahlavi* (*Iranian Foreign Policy in the Pahlavi Era*). Tehran: Alborz Publishers, 1996.

11. Most books on Reza Shah in Persian have appeared in the late 1990s. It is ironic indeed that during the reign of the second Pahlavi, little of literary and scholarly value was produced about Reza Shah, lending proof to the hypothesis that Mohammad Reza Shah was envious of, and had other misgivings toward, his father. The books listed in the bibliography, in English and Persian, provide good accounts of Reza Shah's twenty-year rule (1921–1941), but contain little about his formative years when he served under foreign commanders in the Cossack Brigade. Little is available, especially, on his whereabouts and his activities during the constitutional revolution of 1906–1911, and during the calamitous years of World War I. This is significant because Russian officers under whom he served were the revolution's main opponents. Of special significance is discerning Reza Khan's reaction to the June 1908 bombardment of Iran's national assembly by the Russian Colonel Liakhov.

12. James Earl Carter, *Keeping Faith: Memoirs of a President.* New York: Bantam Books, 1982; Giscard d'Estaing, Valery. *Le Pouvior et La Vie (Power and Life).* Paris, 1988; Sullivan, William H. *Mission to Iran.* New York: W.W. Norton, 1981.

13. In chronological order, the Shah's books are *Mission for My Country* (1961); *The White Revolution* (1967); *Toward a Great Civilization* (1977); and *Answer to History* (1980). In these books and in dozens of published pamphlets of his statements in Persian and English it is possible to discern the contours of his thinking about Iran's past, present, and future. By contrast, far less is available in English or Persian that can serve this purpose for Reza Shah.

14. Pahlavi, *Mission for My Country,* pp. 9–29.

15. Ibid., pp. 35–44.

16. Ibid., p. 44.

17. Abbas Milani, Keynote speech delivered on the Shah's biography to the conference on "The Coup and Mossadegh's Fall: A Fiftieth Anniversary Commemoration." Iranian Asssociation at the University of Toronto. August 23, 2003.

18. Ibid., pp. 126–127.

19. Pahlavi, *Answer to History,* p. 15.

20. Ibid., p. 132.

21. Ibid., p. 134.

22. Ibid., p. 142.

23. *Foreign Affairs.* Winter 1980/81 review by John C. Campbell.

24. See www.iranica.com, biography on Arsanjani, written by Professor Fakhreddin Azimi.

25. Kinzer, Stephen. *All the Shah's Men: An American Coup and the Roots of Middle East Terror.* Hoboken, NJ: Wiley, 2003.

26. Speech delivered to the American-Iranian Council, March 17, 2000. Omni Shoreham Hotel, Washington DC.

27. Interview with Lt. General Jafaar Sanei (Ret.), February 2007.

28. Pahlavi, *Answer to History.* Ibid. p. 134.

29. M. Babaie, *Tarikhe Nirooy-e Havai-e Iran (The History of the Iranian Air Force).* Tehran: Novin Press, 2005, p. 411. This book, available only in Persian, provides unique biographies of the top brass of all the branches of the Iranian military before and after the revolution.

30. Ibid., p. 407.

31. Ibid., pp. 424–25.

32. Khosrow Motazed, *Arteshbodha va Hadis-e Tarikh-e Pahlavi: Be Revayat-e Arteshbod Fereidun Jam va Arteshbod Fatollah Minbashian. (The Generals and the History of the Pahlavis: In the Words of General Fereidun Jam and General Fatollah Minbashian).* Tehran: Zarrin Press, 2003.

CHAPTER TWO

1. Mohammad Javad Zarif, "Tackling the US-Iran Crisis: The Need for a Paradigm Shift." *The Journal of International Affairs* 60(2), Spring/Summer 2007 (special sixtieth anniversary issue on Iran).

2. Abdolreza Hooshang Mahdavi, *Tarikh-e Ravabet-e Khareji-e Iran: Az Ebteday-e Doran-e Safavi-e ta Payan-e Jang-e Dovvom-e Jahani (The History of Iranian Foreign Policy: From the Safavids to the End of the Second World War).* Tehran: Amir Kabir

Publishers, 1985, pp. 32–45. Mahdavi, a prolific author on Iranian politics and foreign policy, was a high-ranking diplomat during the reign of Mohammad Reza Shah. His erudition and eloquence are a testament to the caliber of people who worked as Iranian diplomats in the Shah's time. At the time of the revolution, Mahdavi was the deputy chief of mission at Iran's embassy in London. He returned to Iran and has focused on writing about Iranian history, especially diplomatic history. His first book on this topic, cited above, was published in 1985 in Tehran. His second book on this topic, which is the most significant attempt at understanding the foreign policy of the Pahlavi era, was published in 1996 in Tehran.

3. Ibid., p. 64.

4. See Abdolreza Hooshang Mahdavi, *Siasat-e Khareji-e Iran Dar Doran-e Pahlavi (Iranian Foreign Policy in the Pahlavi Era).* Tehran: Alborz Publishers, 1996.

5. The material here is mostly gleaned from Iran's official news agency (IRNA.com) and from the Web site of the Iranian foreign ministry and the Iranian President's Office.

6. *Fortune Magazine.* February 21, 2005, "Iran Looks East" by Vivienne Walt.

7. Gleaned from the chapter by Afshin Marashi, "Reforming the Nation: The Shah's Official State Visit to Kemalist Turkey," June to July 1934, pp. 99–119. In Cronin, Stephanie, ed. *The Making of Modern Iran: State and Society Under Riza Shah, 1921–1941.* London and New York: Routledge, 2003.

8. Ibid., p. 105.

9. Ibid., p. 114.

10. Associated Press, November 30, 2006.

11. Islamic Republic News Agency. May 12, 2006.

CHAPTER THREE

1. UN press release, March 23, 2007.

2. Xinhua, People's Daily Online, May 10, 2006.

3. Islamic Republic News Agency, May 15, 2006.

4. Royal Embassy of Saudi Arabia, Washington, DC. Press Release.

5. *Newsweek.* March 29, 2007.

6. Gleaned from the Web site of the annual Munich Security Conference. February 2007.

7. Reported by Roman Kupchinsky, March 20, 2007, Radio Free Europe/Radio Liberty.

8. Reported on March 19, 2007.

9. Christine C. Fair, "Indo-Iranian Ties: Thicker Than Oil." *Middle East Review of International Affairs* (MERIA Journal). March 2007.

10. Kenneth Katzman and K. Alan Kronstadt, "India-Iran Relations and US Interests." *CRS Report for Congress.* August 2, 2006. Washington, DC: Congressional Research Service.

11. Islamic Republic News Agency, August 4, 2005.

12. Ibid.

13. From the Web site of the Ministry of Foreign Affairs of the People's Republic of China.

CHAPTER FOUR

1. Afshin Molavi, *The Soul of Iran.* New York: W.W. Norton, 2005. pp. 353–355.

2. Bill Spindle, *Wall Street Journal*. "Behind the Rise of Iran's president: A Populist Economic Agenda," June 30, 2006.

3. Joseph Stiglitz, *Globalization and Its Discontents*. New York: W.W. Norton, 2002; Joseph Stiglitz, *The Roaring Nineties*. New York: W.W. Norton, 2003.

4. Among Soros' most important books are *The Crisis of Global Capitalism: Open Society Endangered*. New York: Perseus Books, 1998; *The Open Society: Reforming Global Capitalism*. New York: Perseus Books, 2000; *On Globalization*. New York: Perseus Books, 2002; *The Age of Fallibility: The Consequences of the War on Terror*. New York: Perseus Books, 2006.

5. Narsi Ghorban, "The Need to Restructure Iran's Petroleum Industry," *Middle East Economic Survey*. September 22, 1997.

6. Narsi Ghorban, "The Need to Restructure Iran's Petroleum Industry (Revisited After Eight Years)," *Middle East Economic Survey*. June 13, 2005.

7. Ibid.

8. Jahangir Amuzegar, "Iran's Oil Stablization Fund: A Misnomer," *Middle East Economic Survey*. November 21, 2005.

9. Parvin Alizadeh, "Iran's Quandary: Economic Reforms and the 'Structural Trap.'" *Brown Journal of World Affairs*. Winter/Spring 2003.

10. Ibid.

11. Parvin Alizadeh, ed. *The Economy of Iran: Dilemmas of an Islamic State*. London: I.B. Tauris, 2000; Pesaran, Hashem. "Economic Trends and Macroeconomic Policies in Post-revolutionary Iran," in Alizadeh, Parvin, ed., *The Economy of Iran: Dilemmas of an Islamic State*, pp. 63–100.

12. Djavad Salehi-Isfahani, "Demographic Factors in Iran's Economic Development." *Social Research*. Summer 2000.

13. Ibid.

CHAPTER FIVE

1. Quoted in Robin Wright, "Iran's Greatest Political Challenge: Abdolkarim Soroush." *World Policy Journal*. Summer 1997. New York: New School for Social Research.

2. Ibid.

3. Eliz Sanasarian, *Religious Minorities in Iran*. Cambridge, UK: Cambridge University Press, 2000, p. 37.

4. Ibid., pp. 50–51.

5. Hamid Ahmadi, *The Politics of Ethnic Nationalism in Iran*. Unpublished Doctoral Dissertation. Carleton University, Ottawa, Canada, 1995.

6. Haleh Esfandiari, *Reconstructed Lives: Women and Iran's Islamic Revolution*. Baltimore: Johns Hopkins University Press, 1997, pp. 3–4.

7. Ibid., p. 4.

8. Ibid., p. 7.

9. Ibid., pp. 27–31.

10. Ibid., p. 34.

11. Ibid., pp. 39–41.

12. Ibid., p. 41.

13. Among Kar's books (in Persian) are *Women's Participation in Politics: Obstacles and Possibilities*. Tehran: Roshangaran, 2001; *The Burned Palms*. Tehran: Roshangaran,

2001; *Legal Obstacles Against Political Development in Iran.* Tehran: Qatreh, 2001; *Violence against Women in Iran.* Tehran: Roshangaran, 2000; *Legal Structure of the Family System in Iran.* Tehran: Roshangaran, 1999; *Women's Political Rights in Iran.* Tehran: Roshangaran, 1997; *Children of Addiction.* Tehran: Roshangaran, 1996. Second edition; *Women in the Labor Market of Iran.* Tehran: Roshangaran, 1994; *The Quest for Identity: Iranian Women in History and Pre-History.* Tehran: Roshangaran, 1992. Co-authored with Shahla Lahiji.

CONCLUSION

1. Glenn Kessler, "U.S. under Pressure to Talk to Tehran Both Parties Speak Out." *The Washington Post* May 11, 2006.

2. Dan Ephron and Maziar Bahari. "Iran's Hard-liners Lash Out at Women, Youth Labor Organizers, Feminists, Party Animals, Visiting Scholars and See Enemies on Every Side." *Newsweek,* May 21, 2007; Robin Wright. "Lawmakers Call for the Release of US Scholar Held in Iran." *Washington Post,* May 11, 2007; "Nobel Laureate Condemns the Arrest of Iranian-American Scholar." RFE/RL, May 18, 2007.

3. US, Iran End 27-year Diplomatic Freeze, Associated Press, May 28, 2007.

Bibliography

SOURCES IN ENGLISH

Abrahamian, Ervand. *Iran between Two Revolutions*. Princeton: Princeton University Press, 1982.

Afary, Janet. *The Iranian Constitutional Revolution, 1906–1911*. New York: Columbia University Press, 1996.

Ahmadi, Hamid. *The Politics of Ethnic Nationalism in Iran*. Unpublished Doctoral Dissertation. Carleton University, Ottawa, Canada, 1995.

Alizadeh, Parvin, ed. *The Economy of Iran: Dilemmas of an Islamic State*. London: I.B. Tauris, 2000. pp. 63–100.

Amirsadeghi, Hossein, ed. *Twentieth Century Iran*. London: Heinemann, 1977.

Amuzegar, Jahangir. *The Dynamics of the Iranian Revolution: The Pahlavis' Triumph and Tragedy*. Albany: State University of New York Press, 1991.

Arjomand, Said A. *Turban for the Crown*. New York: Oxford University Press, 1988.

Atabaki, Touraj and Zurcher, Erik J., eds. *Men of Order: Authoritarian Modernization under Ataturk and Reza Shah*. London: I.B. Taurus, 2004.

Banani, Amin. *The Modernization of Iran, 1921–1941*. Stanford, CA: Stanford University Press, 1961.

Chubin, Shahram and Zabih, Sepehr. *The Foreign Relations of Iran: A Developing State in a Zone of Conflict*. Berkeley: University of California Press, 1974.

Cronin, Stephanie, ed. *The Making of Modern Iran: State and Society under Riza Shah, 1921–1941*. London: Routledge, 2003.

Fisher, W. B. *The Cambridge History of Iran. Vol 7. From Nader Shah to the Islamic Republic*, 1991.

Graham, Robert. *Iran: The Illusion of Power*. London: Croom Helm, 1978.

Hiro, Dilip. *The Iranian Labyrinth: Journeys through Theocratic Iran and Its Furies*. New York: Nation Books, 2005.

Encyclopedia Iranica. Entries on Constitutional Revolution, Bahar (Malekoshoara), Arsanjani (Hassan), Classes in the Pahlavi Period, Cossack Brigade, Education, Anglo-Iranian Relations, Concessions, 1999.

Kashani-Sabet, Firoozeh. *Frontier Fictions: Shaping the Iranian Nation, 1804–1946.* London: I.B. Taurus, 1999.

Katouzian, Homa. *State and Society in Iran: The Eclipse of the Qajars and the Emergence of the Pahlavis.* London: I.B. Tauris, 2000.

Keddie, Nikki. *Modern Iran: Roots and Results of Revolution.* New Haven, CT: Yale University Press, 2003.

Keddie, Nikki and Gasiorowski, Mark, eds. *Neither East Nor West: Iran, the Soviet Union, and the United States.* New Haven, CT: Yale University Press, 1990.

Kinzer, Stephen. *All the Shah's Men: An American Coup and the Roots of Middle East Terror.* Hoboken, NJ: John Wiley and Sons, 2003.

Lenczowski, George, ed. *Iran Under the Pahlavis.* Stanford, CA: Hoover Institution Press, 1978.

Milani, Abbas. *Lost Wisdom: Rethinking Modernity in Iran.* Washington, DC: Mage Publishers, 2004.

Molavi, Afshin. *Persian Pilgrimages: Journeys across Iran.* New York: Norton, 2002.

Pahlavi, Mohammad Reza. *Mission for My Country.* Tehran, 1961.

Pahlavi, Mohammad Reza. *Answer to History.* Toronto and Vancouver: Clarke, Irwin & Company, 1980.

Ramazani, Rouhollah K. *Iran's Foreign Policy, 1941–1973: A Study of Foreign Policy in Modernizing Nations.* Charlottesville: University of Virginia Press, 1975.

Sanasarian, Eliz. *Religious Minorities in Iran.* Cambridge, UK: Cambridge University Press, 2000.

Tarock, Adam. *Iran's Foreign Policy Since 1990: Pragmatism Supercedes Islamic Ideology.* Commack, NY: Nova Science Publishers, 1999.

Wilber, Donald N. *Riza Shah Pahlavi: The Resurrection and Reconstruction of Iran.* Hicksville, NY: Exposition Press, 1975.

Zonis, Marvin. *The Political Elite of Iran.* Princeton: Princeton University Press, 1971.

SOURCES IN PERSIAN

Agheli, Bagher. *Reza Shah va Ghoshun-e Mottahedolshekl (Reza Shah and a Unified Army).* Tehran: Namak Publishers, 1998.

Babaie, M. *Tarikhe Nirooy-e Havai-e Iran (The History of the Iranian Air Force).* Tehran: Novin Press, 2005.

Mahdavi, Abdolreza Hooshang. *Sahnehayee az Tarikhe Maaser-e Iran (Scenes from Iran's Contemporary History).* Tehran: Entesharat-e Elmi, 1998.

Mahdavi, Abdolreza Hooshang. *Siasat-e Khareji-e Iran Dar Doran-e Pahlavi (Iranian Foreign Policy in the Pahlavy Era).* Tehran: Alborz Publishers, 1996.

Mahdavi, Abdolreza Hooshang. *Tarikh-e Ravabet-e Khareji-e Iran: Az Ebteday-e Doran-e Safavi-e ta Payan-e Jang-e Dovvom-e Jahani (The History of Iranian Foreign Policy: From the Safavids to the End of the Second World War).* Tehran: Amir Kabir Publishers, 1985.

Motazed, Khosrow. *Arteshbodha va Hadis-e Tarikh-e Pahlavi: Be Revayat-e Arteshbod Fereidun Jam va Arteshbod Fatollah Minbashian (The Generals and the History of the Pahlavis: In the Words of General Fereidun Jam and General Fatollah Minbashian).* Tehran: Zarrin Press, 2003.

Pesyan, Najaf Gholi. *Az Sacadkuh ta Zuhansburg* (*From Savadkooh to Johannesburg: The Story of Reza Khan*). Tehran, Nashr-e Elm, 1999.

Toloui, Mahmoud. *Pedar va Pessar: NaGofteha az Zengegi va Ruzegar-e Pahlaviha* (*Father and Son: The Untold Story of the Pahlavis*). Tehran: Nashre-Elm, 1995.

Toloui, Mahmoud. *Bazigaran-e Asr-e Pahlavi: Az Foroughi ta Fardoust* (*The Players of the Pahlavi Era: From Foroughi till Fardoust*). Tehran: Nashr-e Elm, 1992.

Index

About the Authors

ALIDAD MAFINEZAM is a Toronto-based lecturer and consultant. He has taught at the University of Toronto and the University of Winnipeg and has worked as a consultant to numerous foundations and nonprofit organizations. He is translator and editor of *Hope and Challenge: The Iranian President Speaks* by Mohammad Khatami (1997). He has also written about Iran for the Middle East Institute at Columbia University.

ARIA MEHRABI earned his Ph.D. in international affairs and economic development at the Johns Hopkins Paul H. Nitze School of Advanced International Studies, where he wrote and conducted field research on Iran's information revolution and its transformative effects on politics, religion, and the economy. He has worked as a Middle East risk consultant to the RAND Corporation and lectured on international affairs at Georgetown University. An advocate on the forefront of the global issue of trafficking in women and children, he has funded programs at the Protection Project of Johns Hopkins in connection with the State Department, educating global bureaucrats on the issues of trafficking. He is a member of the Urban Land Institute and serves on the Leadership Council of the New America Foundation.